Work for All Children

Work for All Children

Terry P. Anderson
Sandra Maslow Smith

 Path of Potential

Work for All Children

PHOTOGRAPHY
Carol Anderson
Candi Clark
Sandra Maslow Smith
Donna Kremer Turbyfill

COVER AND BOOK DESIGN
Candi Clark

GRAPHICS AND PRINTING
Candi Clark
Sunburst Graphics & Printing, Inc.
Grand Junction, CO 81503 USA

STYLISTIC EDITOR
Paige Gengenbach

PUBLISHER
Path of Potential
P.O. Box 4058
Grand Junction, CO 81502 USA
www.pathofpotential.org

AUTHORS
Terry P. Anderson
Sandra Maslow Smith

First Printing - 2008
Printed in the United States of America
SFI ® Certified (Sustainable Forestry Initiative)
Acid Free

Path of Potential is a trademark of TS Potential, LLC.

ISBN-10: 0-9760139-5-9
ISBN-13: 978-0-9760139-5-2

Contents:

Each and all, regardless of where we are in life, can take on and have a meaningful role... a role that expresses our reason for being here... our role in the work for all children.

The Beginning of the Work

Working Towards Wholeness

In our life, we often find ourselves doing work that we "must do"... whether what we must do is determined by our culture, our desires, our habits, or the real and present needs of our family and community.

There is additional work, however, that "must be done"... work that unfolds the potential enfolded within each and all; work that enriches life – the whole of life on earth – and by so doing, elevates the future of humankind.

The subject of this book is that essential work which contributes to the intended upward progression of the heart and soul of humanity... the work for all children.

Behind all that is written here is the essential aim of moving towards wholeness... and away from that which divides. With a bit of reflection, it becomes obvious that we cannot legislate wholeness... thus this work is truly a grassroots process deliberately chosen by willing instruments who are guided by intended intuition, and fueled by love. For we know that if love is not present in the process, love will not be present in the outcome...
and with love, all things are possible.

PART 1 - PREPARING OURSELVES

Reflecting on the Working of Love

Love... continuously emanates from the Essence of creation, its true and only Source. With unfailing alertness and infinite patience, love seeks an opening through which it can flow... the means by which it can enter into the working of the world. In the absence of an open vessel, a receptive heart, love cannot enter the world... and a loveless world ceases to work, ceases to be, and brings unimaginable suffering to its Creator.

Upon entry, love works not to gain power... nor does it pursue power and authority over others; it seeks not to dominate, nor to be understood. Love seeks to illuminate and gain understanding of.

Love casts not shadows... it is pure light... a light that freely enters a receptive heart - a beckoning instrument. Love, once welcomed, goes about its work of reflecting from and among one another... a reflecting that awakens faith, breathes life into hope, and strengthens spirit. Love illuminates ultimate truths... the truth of our instrumentality... the illusion of our being a source... the truth of our oneness and equality... the reality that but for our Creator, no one is superior. Love celebrates our uniqueness as it works to unfold and manifest our essence.

While love holds returning as its purpose... love has as its ultimate aim lighting the path of evolution of our being... the path by which we ultimately become that which was and is intended: a perfect reflection of the image from and through which we were created. Love enters and lights our path in ways that sustain our longing to return, and our ever-strengthening yearning to become. Always beckoning and occasionally admonishing us along our intended path of progression, love lightens the burden of our soul... yet calls attention to and provides focus to the work before us.

Love lights the way... and leads us to advance our humanness beyond love based on or restricted to common or shared blood... to embrace one another, each and all members of the human family, as brothers and sisters – neighbors, one and all.

As we, humankind, progress along our path, and our capacity for embracing the working of love deepens, our work becomes increasingly intrinsic... requiring more inner acceptance and a freer and more conscious choice not realizable through external forces (that is, authority or persuasion, reason and logical argument, commands, threats, fear or guilt), but more and more through the work of our heart and the working of our conscience. Each new progression does not diminish the significance of the previous, nor lessen it being required... rather, that which comes before becomes enfolded into the new... with deeper and truer meaning, and a greater possibility of being truly lived out. Thus the new progression - to embrace the whole of life on earth, to understand and honor its working, and to nourish and bring forth life's potential and its processes - does not diminish the love required and intended between and among our brothers and sisters... nor does it lessen, but rather makes more real, the truth of our dignity and equality. And, as we continue our progression along our path, love's working calls upon and requires many more, not fewer, receptive hearts and willful instruments... especially now, with oneness and wholeness being brought to the fore. These receptive hearts become the focal points of the light, of that which is to be understood and served... the aim of our work.

That which love illuminates and wisdom enables us to see, brings to faith a new dimension and added perspective. Faith which has worked to sustain the path of our return – the path of return to the Source - now adds the dimension of our instrumentality and role in the ongoing creation... for humankind was not intended nor designed as the end point of creation, but rather as an instrument with an authentic and genuine co-creator role... a role in the unfolding, and yet to be unfolded majesty and mystery of creation... a role that requires we become fully and truly human... thus fulfilling and perfecting the intent and design of the Creator... and therein lies the hope.

Purposeful Cycles of Life

Through reflection and contemplation on the cyclical nature of life, some cycles - cycles within the greater cycle of life - begin to emerge... emerge from the essence of life itself... cycles that have as their purpose, essential work – work essential to ongoingly sustaining, enriching and advancing human life, and our unfolding progression along the path of becoming fully and truly human. With a bit of added reflection and contemplation, we can see the relevance of these human cycles to life itself, to the whole of life, and to the community of life to which we belong.

The essential work of each of these cycles becomes for us a source of purposes, of roles we can and need to take on... purposes that bring value to life such that we can sustain and access the will necessary to maintain our presence and commitment to essential processes. The cycles also provide for us an arena through and into which our own essence, our uniqueness, our gift can be brought into life - into life's processes, as well as into our life's work and the working of life.

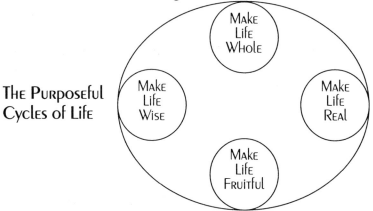

The Purposeful
Cycles of Life

Make
Life
Whole

Make
Life
Wise

Make
Life
Real

Make
Life
Fruitful

Further reflecting on these cycles, we gain a clear impression of intention – of intentionality in the design of life itself. And further yet we see both the clear distinctiveness of each cycle, and equally clear, the naturalness and necessity for each to color the other... influencing not only in ways that bring more vitality to our experience of life, but also in ways to ensure life – human life – does not simply become a repetition of sameness, nor does it drift downward in a regression of humanness. All purposeful cycles of life clearly are systemic elements (not a linear progression) of the greater cycle of life. And while each have their essential work, they seem to share a common aim of enrichening, deepening and enabling our progression towards becoming fully and truly human.

What follows here are some thoughts – a thumbnail sketch of thoughts – that have emerged from the contemplation. It is hoped that sufficient color and character of truth are present such that the thumbnail sketch will evoke further reflection, contemplation and most particularly, dialogue.

MAKE LIFE WHOLE
The most sacred sound is the first cry of the newborn. It is the proclamation of the beginning of another cycle of life. It is the utterance – the voice - of creation itself. It is a pure expression of faith: the faith of the Creator – the Source of life – in the unrealized potential of the people... the potential to be and become what is intended... the potential to fulfill our role in the intended unfolding.

It is through the children that we become awakened to and reminded of wholeness... each child is intended to become whole as a person, as a living human being. We notice in children, particularly the very young, the effort they put towards generating wholeness, and their amazing capability to detect the presence or absence of it. As we go about working for all children, we discover from experience and reflection, the necessity for wholeness... wholeness of community, a community that holds as a central purpose the development of the children – each and every one. We also notice that if the community has little value or regard for developing the children, it is most difficult for family to do this essential work.

MAKE LIFE REAL
Life as we know it, life on this earth, is dynamic, dramatic and evolving – unfolding in an upward direction, pursuing a yet to be filled intention, not the least of which is our becoming fully and truly human. It is into this unfolding drama that the young adult fully enters into the stream of life, the stream of becoming. Here the necessity to "make life real" is critical. How essential it becomes to select purposes and paths that reflect the realness of what is beginning to or trying to emerge... all of which must be done in the context of developing one's capacity to provide for and sustain one's existence... a preparation for what we at times refer to as "making a living, supporting oneself, supporting one's family"... a truly complex and often hazardous purposeful cycle of life, particularly complex because of the need to deal with the realities of existence without the loss of access to essence, uniqueness and a sense of purpose and meaning in one's work and life.

MAKE LIFE FRUITFUL
Earth was created to have a place for life to enter into the working of the universe. Earth was not intended to be a place for a meager expression of life, but rather a place where life is to flourish, develop and evolve... a

vibrant and vital place, a home teeming with life. We, humankind, have a role, a co-creator role, in regards to life on earth… in regards to honoring and sustaining essential life processes.

As we reflect on our path, our entwining path, our way of being and doing on earth, some thoughts emerge. It is natural for us to want to move up platforms of existence – to have a better life for ourselves and for all. Yet we, like all of life, are truly dependent upon the vitality and viability of the life giving and life generating processes of earth. As such, human requirements, while they may be unique, are not separate from – are not outside of – what is necessary for all of life. We, like other living creatures, engage in processes to produce structures (for example,, shelter, food) required for our ongoing survival and sustenance.

Given the realness of that, we are faced with the requirement of taking on purposes that reflect an understanding of the distinct but inseparable nature of our essential processes from the life processes of earth and fellow creatures of earth. It is out of this understanding that we begin to see more clearly the intended notion of "make life fruitful," a notion that carries within it the sense of "being productive," but doing so in a wise way - a conscientious way in regards to future generations of humankind and in regard to life generating processes of earth. Perhaps, by example, more simply stated: the soil our children inherit should be more life giving, more fertile, more fruitful than when we, the current generation, inherited it. Similar enriching notions should be true for all essential processes.

MAKE LIFE WISE
Wisdom is present to creation… and thus has clear

access to intent. Wisdom, through reflection, contemplation and dialogue, is accessible. Wisdom's way of working has much the character of a teaching... a teaching where the focus is on the significant, and away from gaining functional skill and factual learning. Whereas reason is called upon to generate the structures and methodologies required for "being productive," it is wisdom that is called upon to ensure we are not blind to the significant in our zeal to be productive... especially that nature of productivity aimed at advancing our platforms of existence.

And so, as we enter the purposeful cycle of "making life wise," we notice a real and required emphasis on engaging in reflection, contemplation and dialogue, all of which are aimed at, in search of, the teaching – the significant, the meaning of the experiences we have had throughout our lives... a teaching that emerges, not as advice, but rather as a clear articulation of what is significant, of what cannot be lost, of what is necessary to retain even in the new unfolding.

There is another aspect of this purposeful cycle - the cycle of making life wise - that often shows up. In a very real sort of way, it seems to relate to wholeness... wholeness in the sense of preparation to return to the Source... wholeness in the sense of having had a purposeful, meaningful life – a sense there was a real reason for my being here and that some worthy effort has been expended towards the path of my becoming. And curiously, perhaps intentionally, we notice that as we are fully into this cycle, wholeness - the essential work of the beginning cycle – is very present and important to us... perhaps a clue here to the meaning of the wise counsel to become like children.

Rekindling the Process Fire of Developmental Work

Central to the process of moving towards wholeness is the notion of work... work that is related to the bringing forth, the unfolding of enfolded potential. This work, even when we experience it as an individual, is always carried out in the context of a larger whole - something greater than ourselves, often a system, a living system of which we are a part. As such, our work and our purpose become, in many ways, one and the same. This work, this unfolding of enfolded potential, is the process by which we develop – develop as a person, and as a human society... the very means for being and becoming – the way of our calling, of fulfilling our purpose... our reason for being – the path towards becoming fully and truly human... the process, the very means for fulfilling the intent and design of the Creator.

As we reflect on our lives, the life process of children, of the elderly, of life itself, we can begin to see the inherent presence, character and particular purpose associated within and through the stages of life. We notice that even in the very early stages of childhood there is an intent – a clear focus of effort at a particular purpose or work. We see it as we "watch in wonder," a child struggling to roll over... the countless attempts, the determination to succeed. Our amazement only increases as we watch the child exercise this new "roll over" capacity, and quickly begin to work to extend it to crawling... each child seeming to develop their own unique way, but all sharing in a determination to gain the capacity – the ableness – to move from where they are to some other place. It is here that we often begin to see the essential nature and character of developmental work: the inclusion and requirement – the presence – of being and will. Now we see not just the doing, but the willfulness and the generation and managing of being – the overcoming of frustration, the emergence of patient determination, and the obvious joy and sharing of joy that accompanies each successful try.

Now, continuing our reflecting, we can see further unfolding. Crawling becomes a platform for developing walking capacity, walking joins with emerging talking capacity, and a personality begins to show up, all of which become a means for joining in, for developing our capacity for having a role in the family and other living systems of which we are a part. These unfoldings of the enfolded, when we appreciatively see and reflect upon them, take on the character of being miraculous – a beauty and joy beyond the factually explainable. And when this occurs we can, through our participation – our presence in the process – experience love entering into the working of the world... perhaps that is the source of the inner and outer joy, the joy of intentionality, of carrying out the intended.

Upon further reflection, we see the truth of development and developmental work not being restricted to childhood, but rather intended to be present and active throughout our lives. We notice that the work becomes increasingly inner in nature – less external, and more intrinsic. Somewhere along the way we notice that development work – when we are working developmentally – has a reciprocal character, in that as we develop the work, it develops us, and vice versa. And too, we notice that in addition to the doing, being and will aspects of the work, spirit begins to enter – to be more present, more active, more accessible. Along with spirit, meaning and purpose also show up – often in the form of questions about one's own life, questions that seem to increase in relevancy as one ages, questions which, if honored, can be experienced with the nature of urge and urgency we had as a child as we strove to crawl and walk... all of which require the active presence of intentionality, not so much in a goal sort of way, but rather related to being and becoming.

Developmental work does not occur mechanically or in a vacuum. Nor, even though it is inherent within us, does it occur without enablement and effort. If we extend our childhood reflections to the teenage/young adult stage, we can begin to see this at work. At this stage of our life we are really called to make life real. The world we live in is a dynamic, evolving and often dramatic place. The world that is emerging and unfolding before the young adult is not the world that was emerging when their parents or grandparents were young adults. While wisdom is an ongoing need, there is a requirement to develop a frame of reference – a philosophy – that not only enables ongoing development, but also one that reflects the reality – the realness – of the emerging world. In some ways the developmental work of this stage of life can be considered the most critical to our future – not only as individuals, but to humanity as well... a criticality that becomes clearer as we recall that development – developmental work – is the process, the inherent process, by which we advance our humanness. If a generation does not engage in – take up – this developmental work, we risk the loss of development itself, the loss of our ability to advance our humanness. Losing the capacity to advance our humanness results not in the sustaining of our current level of humanness, but inevitably leads to a retreat, a real move towards being and becoming less and less human – a true regression, rather than progression, along our intended path.

In much the same way that the young adult is called upon to develop a frame of reference, a philosophy, that not only enables our continuous development as human beings, but reflects the emerging reality of that which is unfolding, there are times when the people – as a whole, as a living system – are called upon to take up and engage in similar work. Today is such a time... a time for reflection, a time for action, and particularly a time for wise choices. Wisdom is every bit, if not more so, as essential to the called for work of the people as it is to the young adult. The making of wise choices will be greatly benefited by an understanding of the two types of work: arresting run down and enabling run up. While these types of work are common to living systems, the perspective of the living philosophy of potential provides a particular coloring to each.

Imaging the work of arresting run down, we begin to picture some critical elements and see their relationship as a set. We see for instance that this work of arresting run down tends to anchor itself in existence. It acknowledges that that which comes into existence tends to run down, thus the effort to arrest run down. For example, roads need repairing, houses require maintenance, water and air need to be cleaned of pollutants, etc. Arresting run down calls upon intellect and reason, follows a problem-solving path, and looks to analysis, segmentation, facts and proof.

Imaging the work of enabling run up, we also begin to see some of its elements and patterns. Here we, of necessity, work to see systemic relatedness, how each element systemically relates to the others, and how its work and role affects the working of all others and of the whole... a working relatedness that the statement, "If you touch one, you touch them all," helps us to keep in mind. Envisioning the whole, its right and good working, and the systems and systemic relatedness within become primary. Here the anchor is essence rather than existence; potential versus problem becomes the orientation and approach; intuition – the intuition of wholeness – is called upon; and the seeking of wisdom, developing wise choices, and wisdom guiding reason come to the fore. At this time, in the dramatic reality of today, a further demand is placed upon the work of enabling run up, that being the demand to shift – to shift as a people, a people of earth – from being human-centered to being life of the whole-centered. In the absence of a life of the whole perspective, we cannot carry out the nature of run up work required... the work that is absolutely necessary, not only for humanity, but for life itself.

A life of the whole perspective, by its very nature, both enables and seeks the seeing of the whole and the systemic relatedness within. It acknowledges the truth of our design – that we are living human beings, and therefore members in the community of life. It is a perspective that allows us to see the systemic relatedness of today's issues – issues such as environment, world peace and poverty - and to pursue systemic and wholistic solutions and pathways, thus bringing a potential for a real possibility of lasting solutions, solutions which advance our humanness. By way of contrast, if we reflect on an arresting run down and human-centered approach, we notice we not only see ourselves as separate from – outside of - the environment, for example, but also tend to see environment as separate from world peace; and we see other issues as separate from one another, for example, we see atmospheric carbon as separate from estrogenic compounds in earth's water systems. The hazard here is that what gets generated are partial solutions; each "problem" can become a separate "cause," and a source of effort, energy and resource expenditure that occurs out of the context of the whole and its right and good working, often resulting in partial solutions that show up elsewhere as serious problems or issues. With a tiny bit of reflection, we can call upon a wealth of experience where that which we did to fix a problem resulted in an issue or problem of equal or greater seriousness.

Now, to be clear, there has always been the presence and need for both types of work – arresting run down and enabling run up – and there exists within each a real possibility for developmental processes and developmental work. Commonly at issue is the question of balance, and perhaps today the issue is the need for shifting the imbalance – that is, not shifting from being heavily weighted towards arresting run down to some middle point, but rather shifting to being heavily weighted in the direction of the work of enabling run up. This emphasis towards enabling run up seems to be not only valid for action, but also for that from which we take our direction: that which leads our thinking surely must be anchored in a life of the whole perspective, regardless of the type of work in which we are engaging.

And so, as we look out at the multitude of issues facing ourselves and life itself (for example, world peace, energy security, ecology, poverty, divisiveness of culture and religion, and of religion and science), we are compelled to ask, what is the work – the called for work - of today's generation, the work that a life of the whole perspective enables us to see, the work that truly could bring reconciling power, and would enable our continuing to advance in our humanness – to move forward along our intended path?

Awakening Our Yearning to Become

Among a seemingly growing number of folks, there is an experiencing of an inner stirring - an awakening, a seeking, a questioning about life... about our life. Is it really only about stuff and style? Is there not something deeper – more meaningful? Are we not living in increasingly coarse energies – in growing divisiveness? Should not the negativity – even among those who seem to share our views and opinions – be a source of concern? Is the path we are on truly leading to peace, harmony and rightful living?

The heart, our hearts, are being awakened and made aware. Regardless of factual argument, logical reasoning, or justified reasons, there lies within an intuitive discord – a heartfelt disturbance that reason cannot quell. This discord of the heart, when not discarded but rather given proper and serious attention, leads to reflection – to seeking – to a genuine desire for uncovering a new way... a seeking that, itself, leads to further reflection and, like all reflection, continues to move innerly. As our reflecting moves within, we begin to see and discover an urge – a deep yearning to become. Our yearning to become seems to be similar to and as strong as our longing to return... the longing we have to return to our Source, the Source of creation... that longing to return home to a place of peace, love and contentment, a place free of earthly struggle and foibles.

This urge, this yearning to become, is what is behind the stirring and awakening many are experiencing. This urge is a true yearning to have purpose and meaning in our lives, to have a real sense of virtue and value - a sense of being significant and of living in a way that provides a substantive answer to these commonly expressed questions posed at the end of one's life: Did my life have meaning? Did I serve a purpose? Did I make a difference?

As we move even more innerly, we notice our reflecting takes on an outward orientation. We begin looking outwardly – opening our hearts to the wonder and awe of the creation before us... allowing it to freely enter and work its way into our inner self - to the very core of our being. We not only see the beauty, but begin to experience much more. What now begins to open up for us is a true experiencing of creation's ever present systemic relatedness - the intimate connection of all of life's members... the roles that are being filled, and the uncovering of the truth that we are called to be active members in the community of life. Slowly, but with deepening conviction, we can see and experience the intention and wondrous design of the whole of creation... an intent and design emanating from a Common Source.

The inward and outward reflecting not only bring us real and spirit-awakening images and emotions, but bring to consciousness the realization of there being a void – a source of growthful tension within that works to cause us to seek ways of living that are more meaningful, purposeful, and intentional... ways that acknowledge our living nature and lead us to more harmonious ways of living, not only with our fellow human beings, but with our fellow creatures of life, and with life itself.

All of these reflections – the truths that we can see and make real in our hearts – come to life and inspirit us as we come to grips with perhaps the most significant truth of our becoming: we are not the source. We, like all of life, are intended and designed to be instruments of the ongoing Source of ongoing creation.

Becoming Fully and Truly Human

What does it mean to become fully and truly human?

We are becoming FULLY human when we are...
- Seeing and living from essence and the truth of our oneness – oneness with humanity, oneness with life, oneness with earth, and oneness with the Source of creation.
- Seeking and honoring the dignity in each and all.
- Living from and manifesting spirit.

We are becoming TRULY human when we realize...
- We are not the source, but rather the instruments.
- We are members of life – and as members, we must embrace the cycles and stages of life (of our lives) and the realness of death.
- We have roles to play, work to do – thus purpose and meaning.
- We each are unique - having potential to be realized.
- We have within the capacity to access and manifest spirit.
- We are capable of understanding the intent and design.
- Inner and outer peace are both realizable and intended.
- We, humankind, are not the center of all, but an essential part of life of the whole and the whole of life on this earth.

Meditations on the Essence of Children

The most sacred sound is the first cry of the newborn. It is the proclamation of the beginning of another cycle of life. It is the utterance – the voice – of creation itself. It comes to us through an instrument of pure love. It is intended to stir our spirit, and fully awaken from deep within, a sense of sacredness: the sacredness of birthing... of dying... of life's transitions... of life itself.

Each child is born with an inherent urge to experience the sacredness of life, to discover purpose, to build soul, and to manifest spirit.

We are all children of the one and same Creator.

Each child is a gift from the Creator... imbued by the Creator with open-ended potential.

Open-ended potential lies within and emerges through the unique essence of each child.

The uniqueness we experience in a child is their personal manifestation of the essence pattern imbedded by the Creator.

Children are the future generation; they bring with them – within their essence and uniqueness – the intentions and unfolding plan of the Ultimate Source of creation.

Each child enters this world with purpose and intention given by the Creator.

Each is designed with capability of becoming fully and truly human – of becoming a unique instrument for the entry and flow of love into the whole of creation.

Each child is an essential element, intended to play a unique role in sustaining the unfolding creative processes of the web of life.

All life comes from a Common Source, and each member of life has a unique calling.

Each child born into this world is intended to become whole as a person and to create wholeness in the cycles of life.

A child experiences wholeness through potential being realized, and spirit being manifested in the moment.

Children, particularly the very young, work to generate wholeness… and are amazingly effective at detecting its presence or absence.

Becoming whole as a person requires embracing and enabling the realization of potential and the manifestation of spirit within wholes larger than oneself.

Wholeness harmonizes the truth and experience of our oneness and our individuality.

Without wholeness, neither oneness nor individuality would be experienced as complete; both would exist in the shadow of a void.

Wholeness enables living in true harmony – a state where all of life's members resonate as one vital whole in the process of each pursuing its unique becoming.

PART 2 - Developing Perspective

A Time for Accessing Wisdom and Caring About

Intuitively we are experiencing and living in a time that calls for both accessing wisdom and caring about. Given the depth and significance of problems facing humanity and earth today, we require guidance by higher truths than the truths that our reasoning, with all of its powers, can generate by itself. In a real sense, therefore, the development and ultimate expression of human potential must open itself to receiving the energy and guidance of the creative force at work – the guidance of higher wisdom.

Caring about is the nature of love required of each and all members of humanity. The effort we must put forth and roles we must take on within humanity today are at the level of systems; when we care about, we see self as an interrelated, interconnected element or instrument within a system serving a larger purpose. Caring about is an added capacity to the caring for and the kindness to we also work to incorporate into our humanness. Caring about is love manifested systemically between roles, therefore bringing forth the equality of all roles within a system.

To access higher wisdom and to live with caring about each and all, we shift from our human-centered way of thinking to a life of the whole-centered way of thinking. We find we must "look up" for guidance as we work to actualize self and to act wisely so that our development is aimed at achieving higher order ends that are good and right for the whole as well as for each and all of its parts. We can get a slight sense or perspective of this life of the whole-centered philosophy if we reflect on some of the principles that have been effective in community repotentialization work (for example, community is the smallest whole; come from the heart; take all issues to essence; seek wholistic approaches rather than partial solutions; pursue that which vitalizes all). It is also apparent that this shift from a human-centered to a life of the whole-centered way of thinking requires that we work to become fully human – to fully realize our human potential. An expression that captures this sense is "Living out the intent and design of the Creator"... whether we know the Creator as a being or as an Ultimate Source.

As we reflect on what has and needs to occur in this time of accessing higher wisdom and caring about the whole of life, we can appreciate the implications to any-one or to any entity that desires to participate in or con-tribute to the bringing about and realization of this new level of humanity. One implication is the need to become instruments for the work and working of the creative force that is entering or trying to enter into the life processes of earth - particularly the human life processes. To become instruments requires we turn away from the notion that we are the source and from thinking of ourselves hierarchically or positionally, and instead, take on roles of equality sourced in one Common Creator. As with all roles, there is a require-ment to come from and bring to the process the gifts of our uniqueness and essence; in other words, to listen for and answer the call that reflects the intent behind our essential design.

It is critical to remember that all roles have an upward looking character to them; that is, each is attentive to and strives to co-operate with the higher truths that are both operating and trying to become operational. Through the right working of this process, the need for philosophy and disciplined work emerges. Roles themselves are essential and critical, but neither a role nor the entity that occupies a role can be central; what become central are the life-giving systems and the life-generating processes of earth. Earth is in an ongoing process of being created. Earth must, as a creation, sustain its capacity to enable the life force to bring into being its evolutionary structures – one of which is humankind. Individually and collectively, we are being called upon to bring forth and exercise the potential that lies within the design of the human. This comes with the requirement that the design itself be guided by the intent of the Designer; it is not our own wish or will, but the wish and will of the Creator... thus the need for us to "look up" for guidance in our living processes. In this sense, what we tune into is every bit as important as the "intuitive antenna" itself.

Being aware of living in the time of accessing higher wisdom and caring about life of the whole is an elevating source of hope. We begin to see the potential and the possibilities that are contained within each and all. On the one hand, we experience the excitement of this new way and its accompanying enrichment to all life; on the other hand, we grasp the degree and significance of this dynamic shift and the immensity of its impact and effect on individuals, organizations, communities and on the associated processes, systems and structures. At a time when we are aware of the escalation of coarse energies and mechanicalness within our society, and are witnessing the effect of "economics over all" spreading beyond our businesses and industries to our other societal core processes (for example, educating and parenting), we see that what is coming into existence provides a rich supportive context for any and all work to repotentialize our communities and all essential life and work processes.

Embracing Our Instrumentality

As we sit and watch the sun rise and glimmer over a beautiful bay, we realize the blessings of a life filled with awareness and appreciation of both the word and the works. Through revelation of the word, we are given guidance that surely would be slow in coming were our only source the contemplation of the working of the life processes of earth and the universe. For one, we would perhaps never "see" there is one and only one Creator, the direct and immediate implication being that each and all have integrated purposes – purposes that emanate from the intent of the one Creator, and unfold through the Creator's designs. Common purpose of life on earth, purpose that encompasses each of us – each human being – and all of us – all of humankind – tells us there are roles to fill and work to be done in perfect harmony and in service of the larger whole of earth itself... one Creator... one integrated whole purpose with all parts having unique and essential roles to fill within that purpose.

Given our tendencies - the tendency to be reactive, defensive and protective, and the tendency to place the position of each in a hierarchy of all (unfortunately with installed at the top of the hierarchy, yet another human being) - without the word, without revelation, we might fail to see that we are all one family; we, the human race, are one body; we are all brothers and sisters with a Common Creator; there is only one true hierarchy which is the Creator, and then there is all else. We, humankind, are not a pyramid of power, but a line of equal persons, each with unique potential and dignity, each with a role in fulfilling the ongoing creation of life of the whole.

The works of the Creator provide for us a second route to the truths of the Creator. We have been given the gifts of reflection and contemplation, gifts through which that which is taken in through the senses may be again brought together into one singular integrated living whole of which we are a part. For through contemplating for example, the awe of a sunrise over the bay with the beginning of another dependable cycle of day to night, with all the splendor of nature manifesting itself, with fish jumping, birds soaring and singing, clouds breaking, dew glistening... through the true experiencing of the works of the Creator, true in the sense of taking them into ourselves for reflection, we come to see the truth of the intended wholeness of life on earth, a truth that calls upon us to find and fill our roles here, roles that surely expect we will join with the working of the life processes themselves such that they will continue in their ongoing creation and advancement. We are potential and intended instruments of the Creator in the work and working of life on earth. We have choice; we can choose to serve only humankind and the comforts and pleasures of humankind's existence, or we can choose to become vessels of love, vessels through which the purposes of the Creator may be fulfilled... purposes of humankind relative to earth and purposes of earth relative to the whole of creation... and the irony is, that only by a resounding "yes," only by accepting and embracing our instrumentality – our work as vessels of love – do we become truly free, do we fulfill our enfolded potential, do we manifest the dignity of the human being... only by embracing our instrumentality, do we play an active role in our becoming fully and truly human. Yes, the word and the works are the means by which the Creator touches us, the gifts of the Creator that lead us to the unfolding of the enfolded potential – not only our potential, but the potential of life itself.

Prayer along the Path
of Our Becoming

Since the earliest of days, prayer has been an essential component of human life and work. It has been a constant companion along our evolutionary path... a path that has as its aim the fulfillment of the intent of our Creator, and the realization of the potential that lies within our design. This path – regardless of our seemingly unending capacity to wander from it – is the path of our becoming. It is the means by which we can become fully and truly human... and by so doing, become able to fulfill humankind's role in the whole of life and the unfolding intent of the Creator. This is the path of the development of our being. The trace of this path is markedly different from the path we trace from the perspective of our physical and functional evolution, or the progression brought about by humankind's inventiveness.

Along the way, it has been common to turn our hearts and minds in prayerful, hopeful petitions to a Source higher than ourselves. Our prayers have addressed a multitude of subjects, not the least of which have been salvation, peace, health, safety, a good life, favorable treatment, thanks, adoration and appreciation. Regardless of subject matter, we can, through reflection, see the common elements or the essence of the process of our praying. This form of prayer involves the opening up of one's heart in a soulful petitioning of or heartfelt connecting and interacting with the Creator as we aim to make possible right and good actions and outcomes. It seems that when we are truly praying, we are trying to cooperate with the working of the will of the Creator –

fulfilling it... rather than our wishes.

In this, a time of particular emphasis on our need to become, there is emerging a process or form of prayer that is distinctive from, and additive to, the form of prayer that has been common and commonly experienced. This form comes about as a result of our being called – individually, as communities, and particularly as the whole of humanity – to work and become the instruments we are intended to be for the whole of life... not only in the context of human to human, but also in the working of life itself.

The process for "prayer of becoming" is one that requires we organize ourselves – innerly structure ourselves - such that essence energies can flow into and through us. This flow is an act of conscience, thus an act of the heart rather than the mind. If conscience is present, the will of the Creator can enter into and flow through what is now an instrument... and wisdom can become present. What then unfolds before us is a depth of understanding not possible through ordinary means – understanding beyond even that which is available to the fully conscious mind. From this come a seemingly miraculous shift in transformed individuals and an elevation of the platform upon which life operates, allowing the carrying out of that which was previously impossible.

The "prayer of becoming" has a more active nature - a work sense about it - that is quite different from the common prayer; in this form of prayer, we must work to connect to, remove the occlusion from, and make present the essence energies of our surrounding socio-eco system and the particular life and/or society core processes. If we reflect on Mother Teresa's process when called to work in a Russian hospital, we can see an example of contrasting common prayer and becoming prayer. Common prayer may have taken the form of a prayer vigil outside of the hospital, petitioning for right and good action. The prayer of becoming in which she participated took the form of cleaning the toilets. One would certainly expect Mother Teresa to be engaged in both forms of prayer.

Further reflection allows us to see that common prayer is in reality a "prayer *for* humanity." This is the process by which the people petition the Creator in regard to the longings, cares and concerns of humanity. The "prayer of becoming" is in reality a "prayer *of* humanity." This is a process by which we innerly organize ourselves to engage in the work of being the instruments we were designed and intended to become. Here our petitions include and extend beyond humanity to the whole of life and the taking on of the evolutionary role of humankind – a multifaceted role that impacts all of life individually, communally and wholistically.

Being and Becoming Spiritual

We often run into and get to know people who, by their own genuine sense of themselves and our experience of them, can with fair authenticity say, "I'm not religious, but I am spiritual."

What readily shows up as we begin to reflect on religion and spirituality is the reality of, at least from the experience of life and our interactions with others, there being a distinctive difference - unique differentiating characteristics - between "being religious" and "being spiritual"… not necessarily being mutually exclusive, one to the other, but a perceivable difference nonetheless. It is this distinctiveness, the uniqueness of each, their complementary nature, and the potential for oneness or shared unity that is the reflective source point for this writing.

Before we start down this path, it is important and quite useful to get ourselves organized and oriented for the journey. As is our custom, we will endeavor to write reflectively and from the perspective of potential. Writing reflectively, we are seeking essence and working to see the whole and the right and good relatedness and working of its systemic elements – a more real and hopefully truthful image. Coming from the perspective of potential, we are remembering the open-endedness of truth – its nature and capacity to be forever deepened, developed and evolved.

This journey of reflection on religion and spirituality takes us along the path of faith and the living philosophy of potential. As we walk this path, we will work to filter out - keep from entering into the writing - any angst that may show up from frustrations that have emerged from life experiences of these two subjects – faith and philosophy… trees we have bumped into, if you like. In many ways this journey has the feel of excursions into the high country of Wyoming, for there is certainly a need to get to the high country – to go above the tree line. We are sure there will be a few large boulder fields to negotiate, no doubt an icy stream or two to cross, and some wanderings and retracing of path… but buoyed by the faith of past experiences, good fortune, and right receptivity, we have every reason to expect the journey to be worthwhile, and so…

Let us begin with a few thoughts on faith and the living philosophy of potential. Faith relates to the "hearing of truths." It anchors itself to the directly revealed - the direct revelation of truths through the spoken word. The living philosophy of potential works at the "seeing of truths." It works at bringing meaning and purpose to our lives through the seeing of the intuitively knowable, experientially perceivable truths of our living existence – the truths of the works. In contrast to traditional philosophies, the living philosophy of potential anchors itself in the truths of our living nature and of there being intent and design behind the whole of creation. With faith – the hearing of truths – often comes the word obedience, a characteristic of following faith. With living philosophy – the seeing of truths – the companion word is discipline, a necessary characteristic for a practiceable living philosophy.

The notion of holy, or "being holy," readily comes to mind as we consider the notion of "being religious." Religious practice however, in and of itself, is not the source of holiness. Religious practices can be and are intended to be instruments, true aids in our being holy. Holiness itself is dependent upon and is a manifestation of the relationship we have with our Creator. If we extend the relationship or being aspect of holiness to include will and willfulness, we can see holiness is also dependent upon the relatedness we have with our Creator, some of which is captured in the expression "not my will, but "Thy Will""… the relatedness that is further amplified and deepened by acknowledgement and embracement of the truth that we are not the source, but rather intended to be instruments. This process of surrendering to our instrumentality not only brings authenticity to our "holiness," but unfolds and reveals an additional reality, that being that we are also not the source of love, truth, or good, but rather vessels into and through which such can flow. The notions of the truth regarding our not being the source and the truth of our instrumentality are shared by faith and the living philosophy of potential. Thus they represent points or aspects of oneness and unity. An image of complementary peaks – not unlike the Grand Teton – is beginning to emerge.

Shifting our focus to living philosophy – the spirit side, the side of "I'm spiritual" - and reflecting on others and ourselves when we feel spirited, we notice some things… things like the clarity of life purpose, an understanding of life's working, and an openness to experiencing life – to being present to it and present within it… things that seem to accompany the experience of and the manifestation of spirit. There is a writing that further amplifies our images and understanding of the working of spirit. Even its title, "Life-Giving Joy of Spirit,"* adds to our depiction. We have extracted a few lines for our reflection:

*"Gifts of the Spirit," Path of Potential, Grand Junction, CO, 2004, P.90.

"Spirit brings life to our life, for Spirit is the Life Force – the Source of all life.
Spirit is the way to see the truth of our existence. It is the Source of meaning and purpose for our lives and for the whole of life.
Spirit is wisdom in action – the means for fulfilling the will of our Creator.
Spirit brings questioning that builds hope and dissipates despair.
Wherever spirit is manifested, so too is life present.
A spirit manifested awakens and evokes spirit within all it enters."

One image of being spiritual that emerges is that of standing with one's face full to the sun, wind blowing through one's hair... while willfully, joyfully stepping deeply into the stream of life – seeking purpose, fulfilling essential roles, pursuing and carrying out one's heartfelt work - all the while resisting the seductive comfort of retreat and mechanicalness.

Reflecting further we can see spirit and purpose – purpose and spirit – intimately and inseparably entwined, held together by meaning, meaningfulness and willfulness. We see the perspective and living philosophy of potential seeking to see essence - the will pattern, the pattern of intent, that from which being emerges, that which particularizes the manifestation of the spirit. And so we can see - at least begin to see - that the living philosophy of potential which seeks to bring meaning and purpose to our living existence is brought to life by and nourished by spirit, by the Spirit. At the same time the living philosophy enables the orientation and discipline to open our hearts for Spirit to enter and to be manifested.

Our reflections bring us to another seeking question –

the question of raising of our children relative to their spirit and to being spirited or spiritual as we are beginning to understand it. In that regard, these guiding thoughts show up: Protect the spirit aspect of our parenting; be ever watchful of processes that diminish spirit. As we go about the shaping and educating of our children – the teaching of values and behaviors – be watchful for conformance demands not related to essential values. Remember that courage and confidence verses coddling and conformance are critical elements of the character required to walk the spirited path. Guiding our children to meaningful work and seeing the meaning in work, to having a sense of purpose and the ableness to develop purpose, and to envisioning and developing aim – a thrust toward being and becoming – also come to mind. And finally, remember that our children will be, as all of us are, confronted with the question, "Are we to be externally defined or intrinsically expressed?"

Leaving now the high, treeless valley, the immense open space, the place where ponds reside and the streams bubble and gurgle with a clarity of voice, we move upwards, up the steep slopes toward the peaks - the highest of places, the places where the snow hardly ever melts such that the snow that lies underneath that which we see can be quite old, decades or centuries, or perhaps even older. A realization and reflection turns our minds towards that which has come before, the history of human experience, a history that has a clear and distinct demarcation brought about by the "Christ Event," the oft called "Time of Christ." Recalling some of the history of the pre-Christ era, we remember the conversational nature of that time: God was speaking to the people. The spoken word of faith was being enunciated. Commands, commandments, and covenants – obedience and disobedience – were present. The people were experiencing the real consequences – both good and bad – of particular behaviors. Thus there were "times of plenty and joy" and "times of scarcity and suffering." Then by a willful act, a conscious and courageous act of choice, a surrendering YES by a woman called Mary, Jesus who was to become the Christ, entered into the world of human experience. From the perspective of faith, prophecies were fulfilled; redemption and salvation – a reconnection, an opening of the way of return to the Source – were realized. A new message, an inner process of love and peace, was delivered. A new way of being was made visible, knowable and possible. Seen more clearly, perhaps, from the perspective of the living philosophy of potential, a Spirit was manifested. This Christ Impulse, an impulse that enfolded the previous right and good within it, an impulse of love, peace and harmony, was embedded in the life processes of earth, and as such is accessible to each and all of humanity. Now whereas faith might joyfully reflect on this goodness of peace and love and clearly see it as the "New Covenant," the living philosophy would rejoice in the reality that love was now firmly embedded in the process of life, and therefore ongoingly available to the process of our becoming fully and truly human. Now it is possible to realize our potential, to fulfill our Creator's intention that we become fully and truly human. Now that which has been made available makes possible, through our surrendering receptivity, the presence of love in our processes, a necessary condition if we are to progress - progress along the path of our humanness… a truthful reality that allows us to say, with the courage and conviction of Mary, if love is not present in the process, it will not be present in the outcome. We will not progress if we seek to bring about change, change for the better, upward change towards increased humanness, unless love is in the process. Through reflecting on experience we can see that when love is not in the process, that which we sought to change shows up again, and again, and again, often in a different form. It is as if the "devil" so-to-speak rises up and bites us twice... at least twice.

Now, that was quite a climb, a worthy climb, but a strenuous one... one that brought to the fore another seeking question; can we be both holy and spiritual? Can faith and the living philosophy of potential work together in loving harmony such that we can be and become holy and spiritual? And then, why would we ask such questions or for that matter, desire for it to occur? Well, it is common for human beings to experience, deep within, both a longing to return – to return home, to the place of our origin, to the Source - and to experience a yearning to become – to discover and fulfill our purpose (our work), to take on meaningful and essential roles, to truly experience life, to become that which was intended, and to contribute to our (humanity's) becoming more fully and truly human. There surely seems to be inbuilt within us these complementary wishes – wishes, the fulfillment of which would bring about a degree and sense of wholeness not otherwise possible. Perhaps the realization - the potential realization - of wholeness, with its characteristic absence of divisive fractionation, is sufficient to sustain our seeking and pursuit of a way to bring this about.

Let us start with some of which we know, including that which is experientially verifiable. At essence, faith and the living philosophy - the organized thought bases behind the processes of being holy and being spiritual - have much in common. There is much harmony between faith and the perspective of potential. One holds a singular Common God, the other a singular

Common Source of creation. The notion of commands, commandments and covenants enunciated by God is harmonious with the revelation through intuitive wisdom of the intention and design of the Creator's works. Love and peace among humanity harmonizes with love in the process and living in harmony with the life processes of earth and the whole of life. What is beginning to emerge now is the envisionment of a single peak – a peak with two distinctive sides, partnering one with the other. Faith provides a means by which holiness can be achieved. Some of us, hopefully most of us, either directly or indirectly have experienced people who were holy... and we have known people who were spiritual. We also know the living philosophy of potential enables us to access and manifest spirit - to see, tune into, and harmonize with essence and virtue, the virtue of the land for example. And so, while both have within them what we are asking for, they also share the hazard of occlusion; they both are subject to being occluded. We know that we can create structures and activities within and upon the landscape that effectively occlude its essence, its virtue, its intended way of working - occlude it to a depth that makes it very difficult for us to tune into and experience its working. At the same time, we know we can, without much effort, see the same two processes, external occlusion and inner blocking, as common to the realm of faith. For what is true for the land, the processes by which the essence of the land becomes occluded, is equally true for the essence of faith. These occlusions are often seen at work and experienced among our fellow humans, as well as our fellow creatures of life.

Now we ask, what is the nature of the view that we can see from this high perch? Is it a view that is filled with hope, or one that is overwhelmingly dismal – one that we see as impossibly achievable? The answer to that questioning is NO to dismal, NO to impossible, YES to being filled with hope, a resounding YES that would echo through the mountains and valleys, a growing, a strengthening, spirited hopefulness. From this view we have come to understand that what is being called for is within us. We understand that what is needed and necessary is available and accessible. Thus from this view we can see everything is in its place, ready to come together to bring about the next upward shift in our humanness – an upward unfolding of our potential, a realization of intentionality. First and foremost, love is in life's process, and we clearly understand the necessity for our having love in our processes as we work to bring about change. Intuition is alive and well. Wholeness - the right and good working of systemic elements - can be seen. Wisdom can enter and is entering. Occlusions, though widespread and plentiful, have not yet reached the level of being impenetrable. And even though for some these occlusions have become in some ways sources of identity and power, essence is still present and accessible. Spirit, courage and confidence are being manifested. Pursuit of life purpose is becoming more common. Questioning, the seeking questioning of reflection, is happening. We can only begin to imagine what wondrous unfolding will occur as we gain in our ableness to say YES to our instrumentality.

Shifting Towards Roles and Away from Positions

.
___

The dot and the line are an appropriate symbol for an essential truth critical to our time. The dot represents the Creator, and the line represents all else. The fundamental truth being that only the Creator is above – the dot is the sole domain of the Creator. All else – particularly, each and every one of us – dwell on the same line, the same plane. No one person is above another person – we are in truth, in spirit, in essence, and in dignity, equal. Each and all belong to the human family, and by intentional design, also belong to the greater community of life.

We, humankind, have a long history of effort and energy expended to create positional differentiations within the line. It is common for people to strive to gain "higher position," and seek and enjoy the status that accompanies that position. In truth and in essence, there are differentiations within the context of the dot and the line that are both real and necessary. These differentiations reflect the truth of our equality and are manifested, not in position, but rather through roles that are required to carry out our work of sustaining and advancing the processes essential to our becoming fully and truly human... roles that not only reflect our instrumentality, but also ones that acknowledge the realness of the work to be done and the significance of our part.

Within the shifting of our effort and attention away from hierarchical position and personal advantage towards work sourced in and aimed at the sustaining, development and evolution of these essential processes, life for us becomes very real. We shift from positions of importance to roles of significance... roles that require the discovery and manifestation of essence and uniqueness. Work becomes a source of meaning and dignity in our lives. We find we are not so much desiring dignity and rights, but rather experiencing the dignity and nobility inherent within our design as we seek and pursue the right and good. Structures, structuring and organizing emerge that serve the right and good working of essential processes. Wisdom and reason, imbued with faith and powered by love, are aligned and conscientiously, consciously and harmoniously working with the intentional design and unfolding intention of creation. Truthful, spirit-lifting answers become possible to the innermost questions of humankind: Am I living a life I believe in? What is the purpose for which I was created and to which I am called? What is my role in the work and working of the community of humanity? What is my role in the work and working of the community of life?

Meditations on the Working of Love

The purest intention in the whole of the universe is love.

Love continuously emanates from the Essence of creation - its true and only Source.

With unfailing alertness and infinite patience, love seeks an opening through which it can flow... the means by which it can enter the working of the world.

Just as do water and light, so too flows love into and through any empty, open and receptive vessel.

Love freely enters a receptive heart – a heart unrestrained or unrestricted by the crust of ego.

Love flows within, through, between and among the open hearts of people.

Once welcomed, love goes about its work... a work that awakens faith, breathes life into hope, and strengthens spirit.

We, humankind, have an inherent potential to become vessels of love – to love one another... to love all.

By way of love entering, the Spirit becomes present in the working of life and in the pursuit of the Creator's intention.

If, by a miracle, love enters the one – one person, one family, one community, one country – it seeks to be shared with many, with all: love seeks to be shared.

Love entering always works to build community – to bring about unity and oneness.

The aim of the love impulse is unity – working to unite the whole of creation.

Our heart, when love is flowing into and through it, tells us what is good and right for the whole and all of its elements.

When love enters our heart, we are given the gift of "seeing" – "seeing" the whole of which we are a part, and "seeing" the role we are being called to play within the whole.

All hearts experience deep within a yearning to become that which we are uniquely designed, intended and called to become.

Each and every heart is called to become fully human – to open itself to pure and ever-flowing love… to become a unique vessel for the entry and flow of love into the life processes of earth.

Becoming fully human is not an act of "my will," but rather a process of being increasingly receptive to "Thy Will."

Becoming fully human is an all-inclusive process, open to all of us who willfully open our hearts to emanating love.

Through willful surrendering, prayerful beckoning, and a pure receptive heart, we open ourselves to play a role in the manifestation of love on earth.

Through surrendering our heart and answering our call, we willfully engage and walk upon the path of our potential.

Love entering is the means by which we recognize and realize our potential.

The path of our potential is a community process; it both requires and generates community.

The potential of humankind lies within our capacity to willfully surrender our hearts so that through us love freely enters into life, its processes, and its work.

As love flows into and through us, we discover our true self, find meaning in our work, and experience significance in our life roles.

Whereas the nature of our human design presents to us a myriad of possibilities, our potential lies along the path of intention – the path of our unique calling, heart-felt work, and living purpose.

Purpose is both essential to and the grounds for our becoming fully human.

Purpose brings us together in ways that enable us to grow our essence, tap our spirit, and work for a better future life of the whole.

Purpose brings us together in ways that we are enabled to transcend that which previously was impossible.

Purpose enables living in true harmony – a state where all of life's members resonate as one vital whole in the process of each pursuing its unique becoming.

Living in harmony is a process in which all of life enables the pursuit of becoming by each of its members.

The pursuit of our becoming fully human requires understanding our purpose, accepting our instrumentality, and fully embracing the truth of the Source of creation.

We, humankind, are not the source.

Becoming fully human, we shift from being self-centered to becoming life of the whole-centered, and to accepting and embracing the Creator as the one and only Source.

Becoming fully human is an inner process of reflection, conscience, receptivity to wisdom, and the answering of our call.

Through reflection, we let go of our busyness, attachments, mechanicalness and pride... making room in our hearts for love to enter.

Through the work of reflection, we begin to "see" essence... to "see" what was intended as far as our living and working on earth.

Perhaps essence is the purest form of love we, humankind, can experience.

Manifesting essence is at the core of the work through which we become that for which we were designed and intended.

Work and roles, when they operate from and bring forth essence, enable becoming fully human while simultaneously fulfilling the living purpose of the whole of humankind and its role relative to the whole of life.

Human becoming understands and honors the uniqueness of each, and the living, systemic relatedness of all.

Human becoming is refinement in the capacity of the whole of humanity for love to flow through, between and among all.

Lasting shifts in the level of our humanity are not so much physical, material or functional in nature... but shifts in being.

Only love has the power to bring about a shift in being... only love can shift humankind to a higher order platform - a platform that works for the future of all children and for the ongoingness of life itself.

Love enters through process – not through human hierarchies – regardless of the nobility of our intents.

If love is not present in our process, love will not be present in the outcome.

When love is in our process, we see the world not so much in terms of rights and possession, but more in terms of dignity and potential.

When love is in our process, we create, not as we imagine, but in the unfolding image of the Creator.

The Creator's essential nature is love... and love is the Creator's process.

PART 3 - Choosing Love

The Working of a Working Marriage

Within our human society there are multiple perspectives from which we can examine, experience and reflect upon that which we have come to call marriage. We can, for example, look at marriage in terms of legality, from a religious perspective, from the view of economics or affordability, and from a host of other views; all of these views are greatly affected and colored by one's own beliefs as to the permanence, the seriousness, the sacredness of marriage. The aim of this writing is to add to these views some reflective thoughts on marriage from the perspective of work – our work as individuals and the work of humanity as a whole. This perspective centers around process, the idea of being continuous and ongoing, thus the expression, working marriage. Implied in the term "working" is the notion of never ending or never achieving. It is not a goal, but rather a way of being and striving together to bring forth and realize the open-ended potential of each. The state of a working marriage is quite distinctive from a commonly held notion associated with what is called a good marriage, which tends to reflect an achieved state that one works to sustain. In a working marriage, the source of tension and struggle – both within oneself and between each – is the pursuit and enablement of the growth and development of each as well as of the marriage itself. Again, this seems to be quite different from the common experience of managing one's independent action to avoid serious disturbance of the harmony within the personal relationship.

Before we reflect on the process of a working marriage,

it would be beneficial to reflect on work itself. Work is a fundamental aspect of our design as human beings. It is intended to be a source of meaning and dignity in our lives, the primary means by which we express and bring forth our essence, and the process by which we can develop and realize our potential - remembering that as human beings, our potential (individually and collectively) is not a fixed quantity, but an open-ended possibility.

The arenas for our work are value adding processes. Value adding processes are the means we have been given and need to generate to continuously appreciate and run up (versus run down) human developmental and life processes. These processes are not only essential to human life, but to all of life on our planet. Through our work in and through value adding processes, the whole of life can, as it should and needs to be, get better and better through time. The living world should be better as a result of our being here. Generally speaking, we can see two types of value adding processes: those that deal with the ongoing development of our human society (for example, family, community building, educating, etc.), and those that relate to the materials required for our ongoing existence (for example, farming, clothing, sheltering, healing, transporting, etc.). As members of humanity and as members of the community of life, it is intended that we add value and be a source of run up versus run down; this is a critical condition of our ongoing existence. Adding value to value adding processes is both a requirement and a duty: it is required for us to realize our individual and human potential; and in a true sense, it is our duty as members of the community of life.

Within the context of our design and our work as human

beings, let us continue our reflection on a working marriage. Each of us has a uniqueness, a yearning, a bent, that is present and experience-able within us; this intrinsic truth is part of our individual design and is the source of our potential and the source of our response to what we experience as a calling. Our calling not only draws us forward, but through time, produces within us a sense of why we are here - a perspective that through reflection provides insights as to the path we have followed, and the work and roles we have taken on along this path.

From our reflection so far, we can begin to see that the primary instrument or means we have for carrying out the intent of a working marriage are the roles we take on relative to the work we are called to do in the generation and support of particular value adding processes. Roles require us to BE a particular way, as well as hold us accountable for particular behaviors. Our BEING relates to inner organization of our energies. We can readily experience this when we find ourselves somewhat able to do, but not able to be.

The partnering in a working marriage looks to the complementarity of spirit and energy for direction. The partner seeks to see and provide the energy and spirit that will complement that which is already there to bring about the completeness and inner organization required to fulfill the role. In a way, this process is like one atom joining with another to complete the energetic electron shell of the other, and by so doing becomes complete itself. It is not uncommon for a spouse to see the developmental energetic needs of their partner more clearly and truly than the partner themselves can see. This same pattern holds as two come together to fill a common role.

Beyond complementarity of energy and spirit, roles, and value adding processes, we begin to see the grounds or basis for a working marriage: the capacity for continually deepening commitment. Capacity considers not just current ableness, but the intent and desire to advance, to grow beyond the current. Commitment itself is grounded in the willfulness to work to bring forth the open-ended potential of oneself, each other, and that which is possible from the oneness two can generate.

The pursuit of a working marriage is love. As capacity for commitment deepens, so does the experience and presence of love. Similarly, as love deepens, the capacity for commitment deepens. Through time, the love between and for each other can develop and evolve such that the marriage can become an instrument of love.

Do Not Surrender Your Spirit

Do not surrender your spirit –
    It is your connection to the Creator.
If you surrender your spirit to existence,
    Existence pursues politics,
        And politics pursues power.
        Existence is not an end… but a means;
Existence is intended to be an instrument.

The Creator's love works
    Through our hearts and spirit
    Such that we can become and be called spiritual.
In this way, we are all equal in the eyes of the Creator.

Spirit surrendered to existence
    Produces a hierarchy -
    With those below subordinate.
We are all subordinate to the Creator,
    But no one, no human is super-ordinate to another.

When we come together
    Heart to heart…
    Spirit to spirit,
    Our essence, our uniqueness, and our oneness
        are fully present.
    There are no races - we are all children of the
        same Creator.

As peoples, we have our ways of embracing and
        acknowledging our Creator.
    For some, the path may be along the way of
        returning,

For others, the path may be along the way of
becoming.
As a people of earth, our common mother, and
As a people of the Creator, our Common Father,
We are being called to come together on the path of life.
On this path, the Source of which is the Creator,
We can embrace fully the truth of
The word and the works -
We can celebrate and honor
Our uniqueness,
Our essence,
Our oneness.
On this path,
It shall be as it is intended:
All are equal
All have equal access to the Spirit…
To the love of the Creator.

Our Choice

If we choose love as our Source...

> We walk, regardless of the size of our steps, along the path of our Creator.
>
> Wisdom and understanding lie along our path.
>
> Understanding reveals to us the truth of our design.
>
> We see that each of us, all people, share a Common Creator.
>
> Each and all are intended to be manifestations of essence gifts and truth.
>
> We discover the truth of our oneness as a human family... and the truth of our membership in the community of life - life that springs from and is continuously nourished by mother earth.
>
> Through understanding, compassion becomes possible... a compassion that grows through the revelation of the commonness of our struggle.
>
> Compassion through understanding is the ongoing source of hope.

If we choose fear as our source... if we choose anger as our source...

> We walk away from and lose faith in the path of our Creator.

We lose sight of the one and true Source… and faith disappears.

As the light of the true Source dims, so too diminishes our sight of the truth of our instrumentality.

A false light illuminates our path; we begin to see our self as central.

We cast conscience aside, such that ego can more freely pursue and gain power.

Through cleverness, ego generates intricate rationalizations to establish the goodness and rightness of our actions.

We discover the power we can gain through the generation of fear in others… a power and fear that begets further power and fear.

Fear begets worry, worry that further diminishes our faith in the intent and design of the Creator… a fear and worry that draws us to the illusionary promises of those who would act as if they are the source.

If we choose anger and fear as our source, we lose true faith and real hope… and we hazard the heart turning to hate.

Reconcile All That Which Divides

At a recent community dialogue gathering in Kennett Square, PA*, we reflected on the following words:

If love is not present in the process,
love will not be present in the outcome.

Demonizing, attacking, defending and justifying are
not the ways of love, of intuition, of wholeness...
they are not ways leading to the planetary ethics
we now need.

With love flowing into and through our hearts,
the ethics we create will be whole...
they will be planetary...
and they will be sourced in virtue.

If love is not present in the process,
love will not be present in the outcome.

Since then, we have been reflecting on a particular experience we had during the meeting. The experience - which was one of being innerly moved - occurred when one woman said, "See God in everyone; that's a good place to start." We were not only touched by that statement, but deeply moved, in a joyous sort of way... and remembering that at times of being "innerly moved" (whether our attention to the moment is awakened by anger, sadness, joy or whatever), there often lies within a taste of some form of clue regarding our innermost, essential self - a response emanating from our essence,

See "Becoming; Right for the Heart... Good for the Whole," Path of Potential, 2005. Also visit www.bridgingcommunity.com.

our work or purpose. Therefore we felt some reflection would be worthwhile... reflection that has produced some imagery and insights that we now feel compelled to share.

Our reflecting naturally began with the starting point notion of "seeing God in everyone." We were struck by the beauty, the simplicity, and the inherent complexity of the statement... and how affirming it was to the truth of our oneness, our shared humanness. This faith-sourced statement brought to mind a complementary statement - a good starting point if you will - from the perspective of the living philosophy of potential, it being *"Seek to see, honor and enable the essence in each and all,"* where essence is the pattern of intention of the Creator, the instrument through which our Creator's intention is manifested. Seeing essence is akin to seeing God in others, both of which lift up the truth of our oneness and shared humanness. Reflecting further from the perspective of potential, the truth of our having, while living on this earth, a purpose - a reason for being, a gift, called work to carry out - becomes visible.

Added reflection brought forth a sense of one aspect of what is emerging in Kennett Square. Springing to life in that community is the development of a common wisdom... a common wisdom that is illuminated and made visible through love, is accessed through the perspective of potential and the work of reflection and intuition, and is organized by an orientation - a commitment to *leading from and being led by virtue and wholeness*. This common wisdom is a shareable wisdom... a wisdom that is commonly experienced as not only being complementary to one's faith, but also one that frequently adds depth, meaning and practice-ability as well... a reality that often generates within an inner sense or experience of being more whole - a truer sense of wholeness and completeness.

As the images and the imaging of the work and the working of wholeness began to penetrate within, a principle emerged... a principle that would seemingly be operational guidance to our leading from virtue and wholeness. The principle being:

"Reconcile all that which divides."

Yes, reconcile - move up - all that which divides; move up to higher order, to higher truths, to a new evolutionary higher order platform of existence... a platform that is more innerly, more truly, more essentially human... a platform created by and equally accessible to each and all. This principle, guided by the emerging common wisdom of the people of Kennett Square and supported by the living philosophy of potential, seems to be a good starting point towards the peace and unity reflected in the Kennett Square grassroots community aim "To become a living seed for a world at peace."

Given this principle – reconcile all that which divides - it is not at all surprising that our reflective path turned towards the notion or idea of race, often experienced as an issue, for certainly when treated as an issue or problem to solve, race has been a source of divisiveness - that which divides. Remembering our reconciling principle - a principle that we experienced somewhat as a command - we began to reflect in the questioning sort of way that is common to the perspective of potential. What showed up was the following truth:

In reality, in essence and in truth, we are one people... one people of earth... sharing a Common Source, a common humanity and a common membership in the larger community of life.

Given the truth of our being one people, we begin to see that the very idea of there being multiple races versus a single race, that is the human race, is an artificial construct, something we have imposed upon ourselves. Why we created, supported and sustained this illusion is a bit of a mystery. Was it a trick of false reason, a means of gaining power, maintaining separation, etc.? We may and most likely will never know. But reflecting on history, we can see the consequences of dividing ourselves into races - a division often accompanied by the diminishment and lessening of our humanness toward one another. We can surmise that given the way mother earth organizes herself in life-giving planetary energy fields and the way in which members of life's communities take on characteristics that reflect the particular energy field they reside within, that it would be natural that some physical and cultural differences would arise within and among the human family. Without much effort we could continue to elaborate on and speculate as to the reasons why this artificial construct – this idea of multiple races - has maintained its presence on into today… a time when science is leaning towards, if not having already arrived at the "proof" of, there being but one race - the human race. Yes, we could pursue that, and no doubt it would be very interesting to do so, but the truth be told, it would not be a fruitful or useful expenditure of our effort or resources. Perhaps similar is true for our society.

This illusion or artificial construct of multiple races has produced however, a real life experience - a history of struggle, anguish, enslavement, suffering, etc. - that carries through to life today… often bringing with it - within the emotional memory of many people - an underlying sense of anger and injustice, all of which is very real… a reality that demands acknowledgement rather than dismissal… a condition that commonly seeks healing, and frequently pursues the path of righting the wrongs of history. Again, one is caused to wonder as to what was the purpose of this experience. Of what value could it have been - or could it be? Certainty of answers seems unlikely. Perhaps this human family experience will be a source of sustaining spirit and energy as we work to seek and live out the right and the good - that which reflects the truth of our oneness.

Now here we are with growing clarity and conviction of the necessity for a new starting place… not a vague notion, but one which we have identified as "leading from virtue and wholeness"… a starting point that brings with it the gift of conscious choice. We know and can see the truth of our oneness. We know the way of "correcting" historical wrongs, and of the efforts to rekindle and sustain the flames of prejudice, anger and inevitable hatred… a way that requires the sustaining of the artificial construct of multiple races. Intuitively - with intuition "enlightened" by real experience - we can see the ultimate destiny in such a way, the way along the path of "correcting history." We clearly understand that if love is not present in the process, it will not be present in the outcome, and that demonizing, attacking, justifying and defending are not the way of love. We have history and current reality to reflect on… and, with a new starting point, we have the images and emerging experience of what can be when potential, the essence of each and all, the virtue of the planetary energy field in which we live, wholeness, and living philosophy are present and actively engaged.

Finally, if healing - the healing of history - is to be part of our reconciling process, would not healing be better served and more possible to occur, if we came together and worked to create and move into a space, a more vital and vibrant space than any that has previously been available, a space - a place - for each and all to be and become. This would be a real step on our path for becoming fully and truly human, our path of realizing our potential.

TRUE AND GENUINE PEACE

If love is not present in the process,
Love will not be present in the outcomes.

We can remember the voices of our mothers and grand-
mothers, "Remember to salt the stew; if you forget the
salt, no matter how much you sprinkle on at the end, it
just never tastes the same." Like the essentiality of salt in
the stew, love must be present in any process that has
the aim of advancing us, lifting us up, moving us toward
becoming more fully and truly human. As human
beings, we have the potential to manifest our essence
and uniqueness in ways that embrace, acknowledge and
advance our oneness. Essence and uniqueness are
called forth as we walk along the way toward realization
- toward realizing our potential and becoming fully and
truly human.

We see the necessity for love to be present in our
processes as we reflect on one of the deepest of human
hungers: the wish and the hope for a true and genuine
peace... a peace not so much defined or bounded by an
absence of violence, as great and wonderful as that
would be, but rather a much richer, more spirited, more
whole experience of being human:
> - the experience of an inner sense of rightness
>   and goodness.
> - the experience of living and working in more
>   dignified and inclusive ways.
> - the experience of a more real, a more just way
>   for all.
Yes, peace on the way toward realization is experienced
as a genuine advancement in our becoming more fully

and truly human.

As we reflect and contemplate on peace, our thoughts naturally turn toward those who embraced this virtue and the nature of peace we long for. Of all the people who have walked this earth, the most notable, the ultimate exemplar is Christ. Christ is recognized, well beyond those who call themselves Christian, as the real and true exemplar of peace and, perhaps not surprisingly, love. There are others who sufficiently manifested the character and quality worthy of being called exemplars – inspiring sources for those who seek to pursue peace along the way toward realization. In recent times, four such exemplars are Mahatma Gandhi, Dr. Martin Luther King, Mother Teresa and Pope John Paul II.

As we reflect on these recent exemplars, we notice there are some essential processes that are brought together in a systemic and dynamic way to produce, not only a base for, but a thrust and upward movement toward peace. We begin to see three processes inseparably integrated that work together in such a way that an uplifting, upward directed, peace emerges. These essential processes are…

- Walking in the spirit made manifest and exemplified by Christ… such a spirit manifested is available to all, forever.
- Holding within the heart the aim of accessing and acting from truth and love – the truth and love that emanates from the very essence of the Creator.
- Intentionally seeking to see and honor dignity – the dignity inherent in the essence of each and all.

One other thing shared by these exemplars is the deliberate, thoughtful, prayerful, contemplative process they engaged in before they acted. They seemed to grasp the necessity for seeing and understanding an essential truth - or truths - that would become the central focus, the very embodiment of themselves and their ways. They truly sought to become the change they were trying to bring about. And too, they seemingly understood that hazard accompanied even the highest of ways... hazard beyond the risk of one's life. The hazard for this nature of way is that those who would embrace it, and walk ever so diligently upon it, would begin to think of themselves as being the source rather than as intentional instruments, true participants, and co-creators.

Now, perhaps in the same vein as "Don't forget to salt the stew," we need to remind ourselves of another commonly experienced occurrence along the path. This occurrence seems to have the purpose of making us aware, or perhaps more accurately, of awakening us to situations that evoke within a real sense of wrongfulness - a strong enough sense that we experience ourselves becoming energized and drawn toward action. Through efforts by ourselves and others, motives – reasons and goals - begin to be generated. Energization and motivation are commonly joined by seeing the need for right-oriented control that shifts the wrongfulness toward right action and the right to act. When energization, motivation and control rightfully work together, we often have a basis for and a direction toward the virtue of sharing power – more inclusivity.

Whereas engaging these situations may be less demanding than pursuing realization, they are in many ways much trickier to manage. This is especially true when we are "called to action" without the benefit of the deliberate, thoughtful, contemplative, prayerful process exhibited by our exemplars. If we cannot find a way to have love present in the process, we know that regardless of the apparent necessity or supposed merit, the "corrective action" will not advance us in our humanness.

Even with all of that, the hazard that seems to be the most detrimental to us as a people, and the larger impediment to our progress to becoming more fully and truly human, is the hazard of recycle... the pattern (which all too easily becomes habitual) of recycling the same situation – the pattern of our inability to move onward and upward. Through reflecting on our own experience (not very difficult, since virtually all of us are experienced swimmers in the waters of recycle), we do see some clues or indicators of recycling occurring. We notice that more and more, our energization takes on a deepening character of anger... anger that leads to disdain, and slides towards hatred. Motives and motivation begin to give way to demonization of others and desire for control – particularly legal control that works to impose rather than empower... and power rather than being shared and a source of greater access and inclusivity, turns toward hierarchical, positional, authoritative power over others. Ultimately power begins to corrupt.

Reflecting on what has been written here can produce within an overwhelming sense that can easily be accompanied by an inner tension... a tension which produces words like, "Oh yes ... but no." Yet in the face of the realness of what we can see, understand and experience lies much hope. We, each and all, have within, dignity. Dignity is intentionally, inherently within our design as human beings. As such, it is accessible, knowable and manifestable. Dignity opens up for us the accessing of spirit and love. It both provides a way for us to break the cycle of recycle, and to take on a real role on the way toward our becoming fully and truly human. Such a role requires not power, but rather an open heart... a heart open and welcoming to spirit and love - one imbued with seeing and honoring dignity... a heart willing to take on a role working in ways that honor and celebrate our essence and uniqueness while faithfully and deliberately striving to stay on the way.

An Emerging Peace Purpose

A purpose that emerged while reflecting from the perspective of potential on working for world peace, and the particular aim of eliminating the losses and burdens of war over oil:

> Work to bring to bear the economic, technologic and creative energies of America's people on the development of non-polluting, non-oil-dependent energy systems for transportation and power generation in a way that...
>
> - the true spirit of America and her people is awakened through pursuits that are right and good for all...
>
> - stimulates and aligns our economy around lasting and higher order solutions...
>
> - enables the discovery of the intended use and real value of oil – that which mother earth has taken so many years to produce...

such that all children, all people, and life itself could see and experience a hope-filled future – a more harmonious existence among ourselves, and with the life processes of earth.

MEDITATIONS ON THE
LIFE GIVING WORK OF EARTH

Our paths are many... and unique.
They are the trace of the process by which we – as
individuals - discover and manifest our purpose, our
work, and our role: the way of our calling.
Yet, there is a commonness – a oneness – that is
shared by each and all:
    We all emanate from the same Source: our
        Common Father.
    We are all people of earth: our common mother.
    We share a longing to return and a yearning to
        become.
    We share a common humanity and membership
        in the whole of life.
We are... one living family.

Earth belongs to the Creator; we – humankind - are people of earth.

Earth is our mother; yet she, like we, like all of life and its members, emanate from a Common Source... the Source of ongoing creation.

Earth was created to have a place for life to enter into the working of the universe.

Earth was not intended to be a place for a meager expression of life, but rather a place where life is to flourish, develop and evolve... a vibrant and vital place... a home teeming with life.

Earth is a sacred space where life works to establish and sustain its presence and its willful receptivity to the life force.

The life force is a particular manifestation of the love of the Creator.

Earth is a vessel that patiently, longingly and anxiously awaits the arrival, and welcomes the entry, of the life force – an experience-able, perceivable manifestation of the Creator's love... an instantaneous awakening within life itself.

The urge, the struggle, the seeking, and the pursuing of the experiencing of life, the discovering of purpose, the building of soul, and the manifesting of spirit... all commence when the life force enters.

Life puts forth an unceasing effort to sustain a state of readiness – a level of alertness and preparedness – working to ensure that out of the myriad of life's possible manifestations, life's potential can be made real.

Life, which holds within infinite possibilities, is imbued with and awake to potential – the open-ended potential of each and all.

Striving to become what we are intended to become is a common characteristic of the whole of life.

All of life works to sustain its essential life-generating processes, to manifest its reason for being, and to fulfill its purpose and role... to become that which is intended.

Earth - the receptive instrument of the life force - is the

common mother of all of life... all of life emanates from and through the processes of earth.

Humankind is intentionally and purposefully created as a member of earth's life community.

The living nature of earth and humankind's living nature are one and the same. We are unique, yet not separated one from the other - unique in role and purpose, yet systemic partners and one in life and its processes.

There is no reason to love one another... only truth: the truth of our equality and the Creator's intention for love to flow through, between and among all.

Love enters the world through virtue.

Our life and work, when imbedded with virtue, become unique expressions of the one and same Creator's love.

The ongoingness of life – its path and its destiny – lies within the Creator's intention and is sustained by the Creator's love.

With clarity equal to revealed words, the Creator speaks to us – to each and all of us who will listen – through the living creation and the majestic works. In this way the Creator's intentions become known.

Our significance is realized through the living out of the Creator's intention.

True joy awaits those who focus their energy, intellect, and the full power of their reasoning toward understanding the intended workings of the earth, its processes, systems and manifestations... for they shall hear the voice of the Creator... and they will experience the wonder of the Creator's intention.

Humankind is not separate from, above or outside the larger whole of life... a truth that does not diminish the uniqueness of our design, but rather increases the significance of the roles we have been given and are called upon to play.

Mother earth's potential is more realizable if the perspective and orientation of humankind emanate from our hearts holding the land as being sacred.

Mother earth... through the systemic working of soil, water, sun and air... nourishes the whole of life.

A young child looking admiringly at a lizard asks, "Is this part of nature?" Yes, it is part of the creation... as are we.

The essential nature of life and its way of working is systemic... as such, if we touch one member, we touch them all... thus requiring our seeking, seeing and understanding of the working of the whole.

Humankind has an essential and critical role in the work and working of life on earth.

Life, if it is to be ongoing, requires sustaining the vitality and integrity of its systems. What is true for life is equally true for earth and for her members.

Earth, regardless of the errant ways of her prodigy, toils ceaselessly... never pausing or resting in her efforts to sustain her life-giving, life-nourishing processes.

The regenerative capacity of earth – her ability to recover, renew and advance – is truly awesome... yet not infinite. It is possible – in the most real of ways – for humankind to irreparably interfere.

Hope for future life of the whole, and therefore for our children, requires we quiet our minds to the point of reflection such that we can receive the gift of an image of the good, right and effective working of the whole and all its interrelated and interconnected elements.

The more we reflect, the greater potential we have for accessing wisdom.

A life of the whole-centered philosophy does not diminish humankind or human life, but rather adds significance to the part we are intended to play in the unfolding intent of the Creator... a part that carries with it the requirement that as we engage in our natural tendency to improve our existence – to advance humankind and human life – we do so under the wisdom and guidance of what is right and good for the whole of life... for life itself.

The more access we have to wisdom, the more able we are to experience the sacredness of the creation - the ongoing creation - and the life processes of earth, all of which are manifestations of the willful intent and design of the Creator of the universe of which we are a part.

Wisdom's character is true practicality.

It is through the development of a "mother's eye" that we become able to see the beauty of the whole of earth's creations – of life's manifestation.

Appreciating the beauty of the one need not diminish the beauty of the other. Humankind has the capacity to appreciate the beauty of all... a capacity that may be unique among life's members.

Earth organizes for life.

Honoring life – all of life, the whole of life – begins with holding sacred the work and workings of our common mother... earth.

Humankind has a role to play, and work to accomplish, in the ongoing work and working of mother earth.

Roles and work are the means by which we become that which we were designed and intended to become.

Roles and work are the means by which we fulfill our dominion.

The essence of humankind's dominion is making real the presence of the will of the Creator.

Accepting and embracing our dominion, we walk a path that enables the essence of each and all of life's members.

The willful intention of the Creator lies within essence patterns.

Mother earth – as an aspect of her life-giving work – organizes herself in planetary energy fields. Each of these fields has its own essential virtue - its own essence pattern.

Humankind, as is seemingly true for all of life, can tune

itself into the essential pattern of a particular energy field.

Tuning into and harmonizing with essence patterns is the means by which we achieve the resonance required to realize the particular virtue – the life-giving spirit – so intentionally available within an energy field.

Humankind – through intuitive wisdom, the opening of the heart, and the working of conscience – can, with ever deepening consciousness and understanding, see and experience the essence of each and all.

Humankind's role is to enable the manifestation and the realization of the essences of life's members, systems and processes. Our work is to willfully, purposefully and soulfully participate in manifesting the spirit of life itself.

Part 4 - Maintaining Vigilance

DeaLinq WiTH THE NoTion of Source

We, as well as the rest of creation – the observable and beyond – emanate from somewhere... somewhere, a Source beyond ourselves... a somewhat unfathomable mysterious Source, truly beyond our total grasp. What is, however, clearly within our grasp – fully encompass-able within our minds, within our hearts, within the deepest reaches of our humanness – is the truth that we, either individually or collectively, are not the source. This truth – this intuitively obvious, intellectually prov-able truth – is an anchor, an essential anchoring point for all of humankind... an anchoring point, a starting point, a common truth for all perspectives. Thus we, each and all, can with full confidence and authority, say "We are not the source."... a statement that deepens in veracity – in the strength of its truthfulness – through reflection, contemplation and dialogue. And even in the presence of all our creativity, intellectual prowess and scientific magic, we find our confidence and conviction in this truth does not diminish, but rather strengthens.

The perspective of potential is one that anchors itself in this truth – the truth of our not being the source. This perspective of potential, the living philosophy of poten-tial, also anchors itself in another truth, a reality of our design: We, humankind, are living creatures; an essen-tial characteristic of ourselves is our living nature, a characteristic we share with multitudes of other living creatures and with the life processes of earth. This truth, like the truth of our not being the source, is equally clear – intellectually and intuitively – and therefore both wor-thy of and required to be part of any thinking regarding the whole... or any thinking that would seek to be complete. The understanding, the embracement of this truth that we humankind are, by design, by nature, by characteristic, members in the larger community of life, enables us to see that we are not separate from – outside of – life and the life processes of earth, but rather fully woven into life's web.

We know from experience the hazard that enters into human processes when we ignore the truth of our not being the source, the hazard that emanates from our acting as if we are the source. Likewise, both through experience and reflection, we can vividly see the consequences in our acting as if we are separate from, outside of, the whole of life... the real and knowable hazard that emerges from actions that emanate from an apparent belief that we are immune – unaffected by – the ongoing vitality and viability of the life processes of earth.

The Prodigal Son

While it is common in life to experience struggle... earth, our common mother, is engaged in an uncommon, unnecessary and unnatural struggle... a struggle that goes to the heart of her purpose – her very reason for being: the sustaining and nourishing of life itself.

How ironic that humankind, the apparent greatest of her prodigy... people intended to ensure the presence of dominion, people intended to enable her developmental and evolutionary processes – the very processes required for realizing her potential, for fulfilling the unfolding intent of the Creator – are, at this time of crisis, essentially absent...

Seduced off the path of intention... locked in unceasing argument and inner bickering – each participant, each side, acting from self-convinced rightness... strong of cause, capable of generating proof, willfully demonizing the other... seeking the power of law to impose one's view, but devoid of purpose - in particular earth's purpose.

What is certainly readily apparent to our mother earth, and equally readily apparent through reflective intuition, is the reality and truth that humankind's current path – our behavior – regardless of the well meaningness of our intention, will not produce a resolution to earth's struggle.

Equally true is the illusion that there lies within humankind the power to save earth. Humankind is neither the source of creation, nor do we have power over the life force. We do, however, in the true nature of systemic working, have a role... both in the sustaining of the nourishing power of earth, and in the realization of her potential – the potential that not only is the aim of the life force, but lies within each and all of its members.

Resolution requires the reconciliation of each and all to the supporting and enabling of earth's purpose... her purpose of being a place where the life force can enter into the working of the universe. Here life can flourish, and through its manifestations, fulfill its role in the work of the whole of which it is a part.

What is now critical - what now is required - is an orientation of humankind towards life ... the shifting from human-centered to life, to life of the whole-centered. With this orientation – with hearts receptive to spirit and wisdom - humankind can become that which we are intended to be... we can fulfill our role – the intention of our design.

...And in this way, the "prodigal son" not only returns to the path of intention, but also begins to fulfill the image – to participate in creation... and become a manifestation of the image held by the Creator - a manifestation essential to the unfolding intent.

Speaking for Earth

To speak for earth is to work to awaken the conscience of humankind to the whole of life, for earth's essential reason for being – its core purpose – is to be a place for the manifestation of life: the unfolding, advancing, working of life. Thus the requirement not to speak about earth as if it is separate from us, a separate thing, something to be saved or rescued, but rather the need to embrace and celebrate deep within the truth of our living nature... to seek the understanding of the intentional working of life – the whole of which we, through the intention of the Creator, are truly a part... to discover through faith and reflection, the realness of humanity's role in regards to the whole of life. In this way, and by so doing, we become increasingly able to honorably speak for earth, earth who ceaselessly works to sustain and nourish all life.

Be Ever-Vigilant to Guide Reason with Wisdom

The human being is an amazing creation. With very little effort, we can see and experience its marvelous nature, its seemingly unlimited capacity, and its open-ended potential. The mind – the human mind – is particularly fascinating. It can orient and organize its energies and processes to generate a capacity for reasoning that is truly awesome. By so doing, it can, through fractionation – the breaking down of things into smaller and smaller parts – develop a breadth and depth of scientific knowledge that is the source of the endless multitude of inventions of our time. As a people, we have become increasingly reliant upon our reasoning, the science it produces, and the technology the science generates. No arena, aspect, or cycle of our life is untouched, or unaided by the miracles of science and technology.

The mind is also capable of orienting and organizing its energies to see the whole of something - to see the whole, the working of the whole, the systemic relatedness of the elements within the whole, and with effort, the essence of the whole. The process seems to be more of an intuitive nature, especially when contrasted to the analytical nature of reasoning – scientific reasoning. Instead of seeking more and more information about smaller and smaller segments or elements of the whole, it seeks to understand the whole, the systemic nature of the whole, and what sustains the working of the whole.

A word that describes the type of understanding produced by this intuitive process of the mind is wisdom. Both wisdom and reason share a passion for and commitment to truth. In the case of reason, its pursuit of truth is aimed at the generation of facts – provable facts - that are generated through disciplined, scientific reasoning, and methodology. It seeks to eliminate variables, to remove disturbing influences, to generate a purity of process, and to develop irrefutable logic such that the results – the factual knowledge – are reproducible, repeatable and timeless. Its ultimate success is achieved when the knowledge obtained uncovers that which becomes law – scientific law (for example, the law of gravity). Reason operates in the domain of the senses, and uses its creative powers to produce instruments that go beyond or extend the natural capacity of the senses. Its outputs tend to be physical structures – cars, medicines, crops, houses, clothes, etc. The concrete - the provable - tend to be defined as what is real.

By contrast, the truth intuitive wisdom seeks is more open-ended in nature. While what it generates is equally clear, it lacks the concrete physical nature of reason. It seeks truth that through reflection can be continuously developed and unfolded – in a never-ending sort of way. Its aim is not a final fact, a body of scientific knowledge or laws, but rather an ability to see and appreciate a whole, the working of the whole, and the systemic relatedness of the elements within the whole. Through this appreciation and understanding, wisdom seeks to develop the capacity to live harmoniously and in concert with the essential nature and processes of the whole itself. This then becomes the source of what is real to wisdom. Its domain is not what we commonly think of as the senses, but rather that which the mind can see… and, in an experiential way, what the heart can appreciate.

Through logic and reflection, we can see and understand the uniqueness and significance of reason and of wisdom, and we can get a real sense of the importance of both to our well being, and to the well being of future generations. While history and our current experience are ripe with examples of argument and conflict between reason and wisdom, in reality, they are complementary processes; like other complementary processes, each enables the other to be fully realized. Reason with its facts has the power to confirm, deny, and enlighten that which wisdom holds to be true. Wisdom, with its understanding and appreciation of the whole, provides guidance to reason such that its processes and inventive output can be both right and good. Thus, wisdom works to ensure that the processes and outputs of our technological society are in harmony with the whole of earth, its living systems, and its life generating processes. We can see concreteness and wholeness working together to produce the completeness of thought required to make considered judgments, wise choices, and conscious decisions. Working together they have the capacity to shape our way of life such that not only we and future generations can have a better life, but all people and all life can have a future with greater potential. Separately, wisdom lacks the inventive power of reason, and reason lacks the right and good guidance of wisdom. Together they enable us to be both smart and wise. Together, reason and wisdom allow us to be truly creative – to create and bring into existence that which is in harmony with all of life and essential life processes.

Awakening Hearts

There is no potential in the plane of argument...thus the need for reflection and dialogue.

Work to awaken hearts...not to change minds; for the heart seeks wisdom and begins with truth, whereas the mind seeks facts and develops what it hopes is the winning argument.

Thus the heart sees the truth:
> "In reality, we do not own the water, but rather borrow it from future generations – not only from our children, but from all of life's creatures."

Once wisdom enters, the mind and reason are freed up to pursue the right and good.

The People's Accountability for Good Science

It is natural as one reflects on science to see the good of science. Science, through its "miracles" and "magic" has worked to benefit humankind in a myriad of ways. It has cured illnesses, eradicated diseases, and through its offspring, technology, produced a seemingly endless line of products that both improve our existence and continue to amaze us. It is a constant source of wonder. No one has benefited more, nor been more involved in the development and evolution of science, than we in America. Science, for us, has painstakingly uncovered mysteries and solved problems that have plagued humankind for generations. It has both fueled and made possible the expression of our desire for exploration and our innate curiosity. Science is the means by which we move into and explore new frontiers. It has become an operating characteristic of the American people; we rely upon it and have confidence in its problem-solving capacity. Considering what we have experienced from the "good" of science, it is no wonder that we grant it such high regard and authority – much of which has been earned and sustained through what is often called good science.

Science, good science, is a highly disciplined, very rational, deeply reasoned process. Through scientific method and interactions and debates among the people of science, it works to produce facts, genuine proof, and reliable, repeatable investigations. It demands integrity of those who take on the role of scientist. Good science works to ensure the veracity and integrity of its outcomes through an open process of scrutiny, inspection and revelation of one's thinking and methodology. This process - this way of working - is what society holds in mind as it authorizes those who are engaged in the scientific role. Society expects and requires those individuals and organizations to be true to the principles of scientific investigation, and to carry out investigation in a highly principled and ethical manner. This good science is not only required for effective scientific and technological effort, but is essential for a society that turns to science for directional decisions and choices; a society that desires to be guided, not by wish, whim or emotion, but rather by scientifically generated facts and knowledge. Science, good science, strives to live up to the ideal of unbiased, un-manipulated factual proof, from which highly rational, highly reasoned decisions and choices can be made. This is the virtue that we in America call for and have come to rely upon and expect.

As we reflect on history, we can readily see how science has affected our lives and our ways of living. Through chemistry and physics, science has produced technological structures (for example, medicines, automobiles, computers) that have significantly and in many ways unbelievably altered humankind's experience of life on earth. As we observe, consider and reflect on these structures and their effects, we can see and sense that these very structures that have benefited humankind, have affected the working of life on earth. In this regard, we as a people, seem to have an increasing sense of discomfort - an uneasiness - with continuing behaviors and attitudes that historically seemed right and within our rights. This discomfort and concern has been exacerbated by the recent expansion, extension and acceleration of our science and technology into the life fields of biology and genetic engineering. This technology enables us to go beyond affecting the working of life and the working of life processes (for example, a salmon swimming upstream encountering a dam), to participating directly in the life processes and life generating processes of earth.

The structures and structuring generated by chemistry and physics are more indirect in nature – indirect in the sense that they act to cause a different structuring (for example, mutations in insects from pesticides), or to cause an inability to produce a certain structure (for example, DDT and the loss of egg shell integrity, thus the inability of eagles to reproduce). Because of this indirect action, they carry with them an inbuilt possibility of recovery (for example, stop using DDT and eagle numbers increase; remove the dam and salmon can reproduce and sustain their character and existence). Processes that can act directly on life itself (for example, genetic engineering) do not have an inbuilt recovery or retrieval possibility. These processes produce structures that can and therefore will enter directly into the life processes and the life generating processes of earth; by so doing, there is a real and inevitable possibility of affecting and altering all of life, all of life's processes, and the life generating capacity and processes of earth itself. The depth, the rate of progression, and the extent of the possibility is analogous to that which our virtual world experiences when a single virus enters, infects and creates havoc in and among our computer and information networks. In an ironic sort of way, our technology has produced the systemic model by which we can readily see and experience through our virtual world, the power of artificially structured "viruses" in the real world of our life and of all life.

As a people, we have a dilemma. We can and often do

experience an inner struggle, a division within ourselves that is commonly associated with the processes of morality and ethicality. As such, we can experience the temptations present in conversation such as, "If you can imagine it and fund it – you can do it," and, "If we don't do it, someone else will... and we'll lose our competitive and economic advantage and power." We are also engaged in the struggle to determine the right and the good. What is the right thing to do? What is good for us, for life, for earth itself? In our struggle, we, as is our American way, have called upon our science and those in the scientific and technological role to provide a sound and objective basis for decisions and choosing directions. Science, as is its way, is engaging in experimentation, fact generation, and debate. The traditional restraint, whereby advances were limited by resources and the imagination of those in the scientific and technological role, still seems to be in operation. The appropriateness of this as a restraint, considering the magnitude of the hazard, is certainly and justifiably in doubt. Unfortunately, justified doubt neither resolves the issue nor does it in and of itself provide a way or the necessary guidance. We can, however, through reflection and consideration, gain insight into truths about ourselves as a people, the right and good working of our society, and the working of earth and its life processes. From this, we the people could determine right and good actions and direction – that which enable us to enjoy the good of science, and ensures we practice good science.

Whereas doubt – the appearance of impossibility – might defeat other people, it is inherent in the character of America and its people that once necessity is determined, whether or not it is possible becomes irrelevant. We the people, our society, have the accountability and responsibility that accompanies the role of authorizing those in scientific and technological roles. While we certainly need to call upon those who have expertise, we cannot abdicate our responsibility for carrying out our role; our role requires we demand good science of those producing structures that will enter into the life stream, the life generating processes of earth. Should not good science align itself with that which is not only good for humankind, but good for life and good for the life processes of earth as well? Should not good science keep, with even higher demands and standards, its rigorous, disciplined highly reasoned nature? Should not good science be guided by the systemic work and working of life and the life generating processes of earth?

What truths do we know about life and earth that could provide a basis for guiding and ensuring good science? Generations ago, Chief Seattle expressed one such truth:

Humankind has not woven the web of life.
We are but one thread within it.
Whatever we do to the web, we do to ourselves.
All things are bound together.
All things connect.

Other truths follow:
   •The uniqueness of earth is the presence of life. Earth appears to have been created to provide a place for the life force to enter and go about its work.
   •Earth organizes itself in planetary energy fields, each of which works to bring about unique patterns and expressions of life. We can readily see this as we enter into planetary energy fields such as deserts, prairies, rainforests, mountains, river basins, etc. When we are present in these energy fields, we can, with right receptivity, experience the effect of the pattern of the energy field on our mind, our person and our doing. A manifes-

tation of this becomes apparent in the cultural and behavioral patterns of the people of the rainforest, people of the prairies, etc. Within these energy fields, we can see and discover a living systemic ordering of the ecology and sociology.

• It is quite clear that life works through planetary energy fields to generate particular patterns of structures and structuring within ecological and sociological beings and systems. It is within these energy fields that steady state (sustaining the potential and working of life processes), as well as evolutionary processes (moving up to higher order value planes), are carried out.

Reflecting on these truths, we can see the criticality of sustaining the life-entering possibility and life-generating capacity of planetary energy fields, as well as the criticality of sustaining the orderly progression and systemic organizing capacity of the life processes that are trying to and need to take place within these planetary energy fields. Upon further consideration and thought, we can see the hazard, both sociologically and ecologically, when we introduce structures and processes that can disturb, diminish or disrupt the patterning capacity of the planetary energy field. From the perspective of life, the planetary energy fields not only generate life patterns and accompanying structures, but also seem to require particular life patterns to sustain the pattern generating capacity of the planetary energy field. In this way, the life possibility, life generating, and life sustaining capacities of a particular planetary energy field are dependent upon the vitality and viability of ecosystems of a particular nature. From experience and observation, we could conclude that socio-systems would have an effect and requirement similar to ecosystems. The process and processing of planetary energy fields seem to be more related to and determined by particular life systems and life energies, than a particular species. The presence or absence of particular species may be an indication or measurement of the overall health of the life systems and processes within the planetary energy field, and we can see the life entering possibility and life generating capacity of the planetary energy field is dependent upon the vitality and viability of its life systems and processes.

In a similar way, we can see the hazard to life, our life, all of life, and to the effective working of life processes if we introduce artificially generated life structures directly into life's systems and processes. The dire consequences of irreparably perturbing the orderly progression and systemic working of life require little imagination to envision. These consequences require the utmost deliberation and cautious effort of those in the scientific role, a firm resolve and commitment to uphold the highest possible ethical standards, and an ability to honor current and future life by resisting the temptation to throw caution to the wind and succumb to the temptation of economic and competitive advantage. We as a people, must also live up to our accountability; we must insist upon, require and support the ethical behavior of all of those involved, regardless of role. Finally, we are reminded that any virtue carried to excess is a weakness. It would be a weakness, and perhaps a tragedy, if we the people were stymied and reluctant to act by a requirement for factual proof of that which is so intuitively obvious and true.

Meditating on Our Work

We cannot have peace without the Creator being a unifying force; we cannot have harmony without an acknowledged Source of creation – of there being intent and design in the ongoing creation.

- o Birds are intended to sing.
- o Bees are intended to pollinate.
- o Humans are intended to advance humanness, to cooperate with the processes of becoming fully and truly human... and to enrich life - the life of the whole and the whole of life on this earth.

Part 5 - Deepening Intentionality

Wisdom of the Children

On Maryland Avenue in Annapolis, there is a placard written from the perspective and in the voice of children:

"Be not for or against war.

*This peace pole made by our children is a symbol of
    hope...*
hope that someday there can be peace on earth.
So do not ask us if we are for or against war.
This is not a fair question...
*We pray only that there will not need to be war to
    protect us.*
*We should not have to live in fear in such a great
    country.*
Did we forget, war once made this country free?
*So, please stop fighting among yourselves and stop the
    war of 'for and against.'*
Spend time in prayer for peace and freedom.
*Stand tall beside our flag. A nation united with just one
    dream:*

May peace prevail on earth."

Reflecting on this "wisdom of the children" we can see that hope lies not in being "for or against," but rather in what we are striving to be and become.

As we reflect on the interactions going on in our towns in regard to issues such as homelessness, migrant workers, etc., we can see that much of the discussion, argument and debate has imbedded within the character or flavor of being "for or against." Borrowing from the wisdom of the children, we can see and understand not only the futility of "for or against," but perhaps even more importantly the necessity for seeking and concentrating on a virtue – a virtue similar to peace... a virtue that offers a true reconcile... that being the ableness to move up, to transcend the current dyadic plane of argument... a means to become more fully and truly human. Compassion may be such a virtue. If in the image we hold for our town, for our community, for ourselves as a people, compassion is an essential part – then compassion is what we should strive for; compassion rather than "for or against" needs to become the source and object of our attention and effort.

Compassion as a virtue becomes a value when we are able to live it out – to live from it in our daily living and working... compassion, being a particular manifestation of love, is not fully expressed through sympathy, empathy, or even in caring for, but rather requires we care about. It is in caring about that we acknowledge the truth and realness of our equality – the essential truth that we are all brothers and sisters, children of the same Source of creation... the reality that no one of us is above another... only the Creator is above.

The desire to be and become compassionate is a commonly expressed intent of great religions and significant societies. The need for caring about our fellow human beings has long been recognized and made visible through lasting teachings; Christ was particularly emphatic in this regard. We Americans, as a people and as a country, seem to be especially called or drawn to this virtue of compassion... a calling and character that has been recognized by others – perhaps no more overtly than the symbolic depiction and words of the Statue of Liberty.

And so, if compassion - being and becoming compassionate - is an aim or is to become an aim of our community, then reflection, dialogue and prayer become the means for realizing this aim... a way of beginning a journey, a way that demands utmost faith... faith that out of sincere hearts will emerge a spirit and understanding that will show us that which we currently cannot see, and perhaps we will experience the meaning of the phrases – *be as the children... seek the wisdom of the children.*

The Role and Significance of Reflecting

Essential to working for all children is reflecting – both as a person and through reflective dialogue. It is through reflecting that pathways of understanding open up for us. We begin "seeing" that which was previously invisible – out of reach. This is especially true when dealing with the significant – that which has much meaning and relevance to us. What follows is a writing that emerged from a reflective dialogue brought about by the death of Heidi, a daughter, a mother's child. By sharing this reflection, the hope is it will create an experience of the breadth, depth and wholeness that comes forth through reflection and reflective dialogue.

Shortly after Heidi died from injuries sustained in a bicycling accident, Heidi's mother and I shared and discussed thoughts about dying and death, including our own. This morning as light was creeping into the valley, I felt it would be helpful to record or re-express some of that which came out of our process and processing. I will try to capture the essential notion or image we generated in regard to our reflection process itself, as well as on the subject matter of our reflection – death and dying of our loved ones and our selves – such that our images can be both expanded upon and deepened at a later time.

It seems at times we were more reflecting together than actually discussing a subject, in that the aim of reflection is not to produce a particular concrete answer, but rather a deeper understanding of the working and meaning of something... thereby being more human in our thought and expression, and more able to cooperate with the intent of the Creator. It is interesting that what often seems to initiate and energize the reflective thought process is a desire for a clear, black and white answer to a significant or disturbing occurrence out there in the world or in our life.

Yet, once analysis gives way to reflection, the desire and need for concreteness is replaced by the vivification and exploring of life and life processes. What emerges is something more REAL than the factual or so-called concrete, much like the beauty we witness in the rocks of a canyon transcends that which would be possible through a physical, scientific description of them. In a way, perhaps it is the difference between having an answer, and being or living an answer. What an amazing critter this thing called human is, when it lives, or strives to live, from the higher and more human aspects of its design, and thereby more fully lives out the intention of the Designer.

As we reflect on the subject matter of our dialogue and reflection, we find we certainly can become wide ranging and expansive: We touch upon many essential life processes such as birthing, parenting, working, aging, death, preparing for death, spirits, spirituality – being guided by such questions as why does it occur this way, why do we respond the way we do, how should we respond, what is our role in each process as well as the larger scheme of things, and how might we think about it such that we can be more cooperative with the Creator's intent as well as have greater access to uplifting energy, and more ableness to live from our spirit?

Now we suppose some folks would not view this nature of experience as being restful, but it does seem that when reflecting, we are being excused from our daily chores to ponder and explore this territory... often aided by the very present expression of nature's beauty, with the underlying impression of intent and intentionality in the creation and creative process, as opposed to an accidental occurrence or happenstance.

An overall perspective from which we reflect seems to be that there is a willful and conscious intent behind the design and construct of the universe. The universe is perpetually evolving, or constantly being created, rather than existing as a one-time-only fixed creation. Each and everything has a role, and therefore purpose in this ongoing creation, the implication of this being that we all have a destiny to fulfill. There is uncertainty, however, and while there is a destiny, the outcome or carrying out of that is not predetermined. We are not just mechanically filling or being manipulated to fill a role. There is hazard in this unfolding, and our cooperation and participation is required, perhaps even critical to the ongoing success of the unfolding act of creation – success being the bringing about of the intent of the Creator.

The process of deepening the understanding of one's role and increasing our level of cooperation occurs through the receptivity produced by reflection and prayer. Reflection does not often produce concrete answers, but rather a deeper and clearer sense of the rightness and goodness of the path on which our heart seems to be guiding us. Reflection is the means by which we can prepare ourselves to hear when we are being spoken to; this is very similar to the notion in the scriptures of paying attention or being awake... never knowing when the call will come.

The other overall perspective, or perhaps premise, that we hold as we engage in the process of reflection is the sense that we can - given that there is intent and intentionality in the human design, and, therefore in life itself - reflect on our life experiences, and gain from them increased meaning and a deeper understanding of life and life processes including death and beyond. An example of one exploratory arena is aging – in particular, the slowdown phenomena we experience that is in direct contrast to the vigor and energy of our youth. It is natural to miss the energy and stamina of our youth. As we get older, our mind certainly is capable of envisioning new and interesting things to do, and often we find we have more freedom and time to do these things; it seems ironic that in our later years, when we have time and space, our energy is depleting. We find that a day in the garden includes significant stretches of sitting (and hopefully appreciation for the time to sit) versus continuous activity. We could have been designed such that at the end of our time on earth (that is, the later stages), we would have more energy and more capacity to engage in even more activities. However, this does not seem to be the common experience, and therefore perhaps not the intent of the Designer. The slowdown, however, is much more conducive to reflection, reflection being the process to produce understanding, which is or can be the seed of wisdom.

Wisdom seems to be essential for healthy and wise approaches to life and living; it is critical that the wisdom earned through life experiences be passed on to, and shared with, future generations. The wisdom that is available to those who reflect on their experiences of life and its processes and cycles is essential to sustaining the process of life itself. It is accessible only to those who have "been through it" and reflected on it, and thereby not directly accessible to the young. They can, however, and need to experience the presence of that wisdom in the elders, for it produces not only a calming effect and future source of reflection, but is truly a source of hope, and ultimately a means of accessing faith and love. Yet, why do we, given this important role, still experience the longing for, and often the ceaseless pursuit of, the vigor, energy and particularly, the doing of youth? This inner division is certainly very real and very experience-able. A part of us seems to be seeking ways to cling to or extend our earthly existence, while another part reflects on life and our life processes, and senses there is an inevitable ending. Could it be that this tension is required to produce a reconciling force within us: a reconciling force that takes on the nature of surrendering or giving of oneself to the Divine intention, thus a true experience and expression of the Creator's love?

What an interesting polarity. On the one hand, we are drawn to continue to do, to experience, and to drink deeply of life; at times, we are driven by a real and true sense that if we do not keep going, all will stop. On the other hand, we are increasingly reflective, trying to bring meaning and understanding to life processes and life itself. We share our wisdom, our unattached observations, and our calming sense of faith (particularly that no matter what, things can and do work out), often finding ourselves working to produce something of permanence or everlasting beauty, perhaps as a means of redeeming ourselves for the energy we have consumed, and the blessings and gifts we have experienced in our life.

Finally, with effort the polarity shifts. It becomes a true complementarity. We have the energy of doing and the energy of reflecting working together - still experienced as separate, unique, and opposite forces - in a way that a reconciling force begins to build. This joining of energies is perhaps initiated by our capacity to reflect on our life free of regrets, and sustained by both our capacity to appreciate, and the appreciation of our capacity to appreciate... these thoughts being accompanied by the notion that perhaps the ongoing act of appreciating the work and expressions of the Creator through nature is critical to sustaining creation - sustaining the ongoing creative act itself. And so it seems at this particular stage of our life we have a part, a role in the ongoing evolution of creation that relates to other generations, as well as the sustaining of the creative process itself. Carrying out our role is much more effective if we can sustain our enthusiasm and joy for life, regardless of our physical capacity. Our demonstrated desire to keep growing and exploring new ideas and places is in itself a source of hope and courage to all who are concerned with or fearful of their own aging process. Again, if we reflect on our design and our life experience, all of this seems consistent with the intent and design of our Creator.

We could view life or the life cycle in terms of the visible portion (that is, our time on earth) and the invisible portion. Our questions seemed to focus on the following subject matter: What is the transition like between the visible and invisible? What is occurring? What is the role of the living, relative to the dying – to those who are in transition? Given that we have a role and purpose on earth, do we (our spirit and soul) have a role in the ongoing invisible aspect of life?

Our reflection and dialogue was not kept at the abstract as we intentionally brought in our experiences of death and dying, particularly the unexpected or unexplainable death of a loved one. Through this processing, we arrived at some points of clarity and understanding which will provide a base for further exploration and reflection.

Being human brings with it the requirement or opportunity to experience the primary emotions of life itself; they are natural and unavoidable. Even Christ chose not to escape these emotions; witness his despair over the death of his dear friend, Lazarus. The challenge for us is to not become so attached to the emotions that we are unable to fulfill our own role, or unable to cooperate with the processes that are trying to or need to take place.

The universe is a magical, mysterious, yet knowable place; its working is complex and wisely and intentionally guided. Its unfolding creation is ongoing and hazardous, and the outcome uncertain; we have both a choice and a role in this ongoing process. Given its complexity, it is reasonable to expect that during the invisible part of the life cycle, we, or rather our spirits, have a role - thus the need for us to cooperate with the transition from the physical to the spiritual.

A spirit manifested is available forever and to all. It is not the death that we seek to connect with, but rather the spirit of those who have died. It is the spirit that we can experience, be affected by, and perhaps affect.

Death is a significant phenomenon and worthy of preparation. Prayer, meditation and reflection are processes in which we engage to prepare ourselves for death. Perhaps another reason for the slowdown experience of aging is this need for quiet reflective processes.

We cannot know what is the work of others, or when

that work or purpose is fulfilled such that it is their time to depart. Embracing life and fully experiencing each other comes to mind as a guiding principle in the context of this thought.

Our reflection did bring to the forefront the realization that significant life events bring with them unique energies that would not otherwise be available to us; thus processing and gaining value from these energies becomes our work. It would seem from our dialogue that reflecting on the experiences of ourselves and others, as well as exploring the thoughtful perspectives of others, was very helpful to us, and aided in the right processing of these energies. It is interesting that the driving force seems to be the need for certainty or concrete explanation. Upon reflection, however, what seems to emerge is increased clarity about life and its working. We can see life more clearly, and are more able to truly appreciate it, yet it retains the nature of a sacred mystery.

With right processing, the good emerges. We can taste and experience life to much greater depths than before; we become able to appreciate and honor all of life, life's struggles, and the life force itself. We are not trying to overcome our sense of loss at the death of a loved one; mourning has its purpose. We begin to conclude that with right processing, we live from a deeper, higher, more human plane of life. If we choose to operate in the world of will – where "Thy will" always overrides "my will" – we can truly view the death of a loved one, our own preparation for death, and ultimately our dying, as means of becoming more fully human... such that even through dying and death, we are able to fulfill our part and participate in the unfolding intent of our Creator. Perhaps that is what becoming REAL means.

Mother's Wisdom

After her recent death, images, memories and teachings of my mother have been popping up, merging with reflections on the shifting nature of parenting and grandparenting as we age; taking me to wondering what it means to "be there" for our children, grandchildren, etc. I have found myself thinking about Mother's 80th birthday, and as my family may recall, a banner saying "Happy Birthday, Helen." It was clear to me from my interactions with her that she intended to have this occasion make notice of "Helen the person" – the person within the various roles (mother, grandmother, etc.) she carried out. At the time, I knew enough to honor the Helen notion, but after conversation with my sisters and some added reflection, I am seeing more clearly what she might have been trying to teach us. There is a person, within, at the very source of the roles that we take on… a person, an essence, a gift to be manifested, to be made real and present in this world. Thinking of this in the context of aging, grand parenting and parenting, and recalling my experience of our mother, the following thoughts show up.

Along the way, there really is a shift in the way those roles are carried out, some of which is due to the reality of aging – physical aging – some of which reflects a real shift in the nature of work and presence called for. The whole image we have of "being there" begins to shift; we can begin to see a transition from being "presently active" to having an "active presence." This notion of active presence entered as I imaged our mother (and our grandmother) as they sat quietly in and among the family – be the gathering large or small. From our mother we learned that this active presence emerged out of quietness, stillness, and upon occasion, periods of being alone... a process of reading, reflecting, contemplating, praying... a process bolstered by reflective, thoughtful conversation and dialogue.

What begins to show up is that there is a particular way of proceeding – a way of working – to bring about this active presence... an active presence that enables us to move into the realm of wisdom... to work toward becoming in many ways a wise elder... a critical role, not only within immediate family, but for society as well... a role that has become less and less common today, and perhaps that is what was behind Mother's expression of concern as she commented that so many of her peers seemed to be afraid of quiet time (of the nature mentioned above). To her they seemed to have an incessant need to be constantly doing.

This notion of wisdom – this shift in the nature of work called for – is again enriched by our experience of our mother's process. Through that we can come to see wisdom – critical to our humanness and to our becoming fully and truly human - is not a thing, not something we have or for that matter something we can gain, but rather it is that which enters into a particular nature of process... the nature of process our mother had developed such wonderful capacity for. It is what so many of us experienced as we sat with her and shared some feelings, concerns, new insights, something we did not understand, something troubling, etc. What we noticed and experienced was that somewhere in the process something entered, not always identifiable as a particular thing, but something nevertheless... something such that when we left, we were on a wiser path, a more spirited, uplifted path.

Reflecting further, it is clear that even when wise counsel was given, part of the magic – the gift – was that it had clearly emerged in the process... there was no predetermined, dogmatic answer. While we knew without doubt that love would be in the process and a receptive heart would be listening, what emerged was relevant to and considerate of the reality of the situation. And somewhere along the way – either through expression or experience – the sense that things will work out, it will all work out, came into the process. The confidence that our mother had that things will work out, seems to me at least, to be anchored in her substantial faith – as well as her understanding of the truth that through love, through God, all things are possible. This confidence, I am sure, was further bolstered by her knowing conviction that as long as she was in the process, love would be present.

As I reflect on what has been written, I am seeing new meaning - a deeper sense of an expression I have held for quite a while: in regards to our life, as it progresses towards its ultimate end, the truth of the matter is our last day can be our best day. I see now that as our life progresses, as our physical capacity diminishes, as we become less and less attached to worldly things, to worldly roles, and as we work to become a more true expression of our essence, our gift, we can in reality have our last days be our best days. From these reflections emerges the notion that there is no greater gift we could give our mother than to become what we are intended to be.

Write Your Own Story

Each of us has a story… and the human race as a whole has a story. We have to "write our own story": our work and role and purpose as they relate to the unfolding of enfolded potential. Our story becomes a truer representation of the intended if it emerges from our initial and growing sense of a calling. Our calling is the inner sense of our reason for being, the acknowledging and accepting of that. It is the best guidance we have for playing the role or being available for playing the role in the dynamic and dramatic unfolding. The unfolding may never be ours to see with any sense of totality or completeness, but through receptive hearts and effort we will be given all the clarity required to discover our path and pursue a path that will enable us to answer our call - carry out the work and role required to fulfill the intention behind our being here in the first place. This is the essence of the truth of what we are working on. Whatever actions we take must never interfere with the writing of another's own story… but perhaps it is justified that we awaken others to the reality that they have a story to write: There is work to be done, and there are stories to write.

Educating for Intentionality

As we interact with young people (and the young at heart), the subject of education, college, the purpose of both and the reason for pursuing them is a common topic. Given the economic and employment dynamics, and the general uncertainty and unease present in today's world, it is not surprising that this nature of questioning and discussing is going on. What seems to be at play here is the notion of potential – of realizing potential... of something including, but beyond that of gaining a good education and securing a good job. There is an urge to shift the platform of our thinking from "what is right and good for me and my family" to encompass (not at the expense of family or oneself), "what is right and good for the whole – the whole of humanity, human society, the whole of life, and of earth itself." Education then, being a common instrument of our becoming, has the obligation and opportunity to take on this work of repotentialization. And colleges, being instruments of our educating process, of necessity can willfully join this work.

Repotentialization work always requires that we go back to the essence - in this case, the essence of learning, of teaching, of educating, of pursuing education... and if we are trying to realize potential (bring essence into existence), we, of necessity, need to develop the capacity for intentionality - intentionality that serves to illuminate the work of our heart, our purpose, our reason for being. Whereas a good job, good pay, and benefits were at one time the primary focus of pursuing education, meaningful work is emerging as a driving force within this evolutionary shift. Again, that which was the primary focus is not lost, but rather enfolded into that which is emerging. This shift - this upward movement along the path of our becoming more fully and truly human – requires philosophy, in reality, a living philosophy… not a philosophy that is treated as a separate subject of study, but rather one which can be practiced – lived out in our daily lives and work.

When it comes to living philosophy, it is important to reflectively ground ourselves in how it works with its complementary partner, faith… the faith from which emanate religion and theology. Living philosophy, likewise, becomes the source or reference point for ethics and scientific endeavor. At essence, faith deals with revelation – revealed truths that seemingly could not be uncovered by reason. Living philosophy, like other philosophies, deals with the meaning of existence – who am I; why am I; what role and work do I have? Living philosophy, however, anchors itself in essence rather than the physical or material aspects of existence common to traditional philosophy. Both faith and living philosophy are based on essential truths, and work individually and systemically to illuminate the ultimate purpose of our existence. Living philosophy and living faith are true partners in that they deal with two of our innermost urges – our yearning to become, and our longing to return to the Source. Each works to strengthen the other; and, in reality, it is the understanding of the one that deepens the understanding and appreciation of the other. What seems to be at work today is that the notions and work of faith and philosophy are becoming less visible – pushed to the back of the stage, if not behind the curtain. What is visible – on center stage, if you like - are the perspectives of religion and science, not working in partnership, but rather fully engaged on the plane of argument – arguing not for role clarification (each do have their purpose and work), but seemingly to gain power over… a notion bolstered by the all too common seeking of the legal right to impose one's position on the other - acting in ways that do not demonstrate an understanding of the serious consequences if one succeeds in diminishing the other. For if religion successfully diminishes or dismisses science (the obvious and knowable material reality and truths that have been uncovered), that particular religion, at least, runs the risk of being reduced to a myth or superstition. On the other hand, if science successfully diminishes, or dismisses religion through the establishment of the physical, factual, provable, material aspects of existence as being the only reality – the only real thing in our world - we lose access to the being and will aspects of our nature, the very source of meaning and depth of our life experience.

Thus the need for a living philosophy of potential… a philosophy that anchors itself in essence, thus acknowledging the being and will aspects of our design… a philosophy that has within it the ableness to repotentialize science and scientific endeavor.

Now, what comes up for us, as we reflect on faith and living philosophy, is a void – the active absence of ethics. The vast majority of our thinking today starts from, is anchored in, economics, rights, or legality. The notion of ethics – the behavioral principles that "we the people" willfully impose upon and require of each other, and in particular of those who occupy critical roles in essential systems and institutions – is not a common starting point for our thinking and acting. In a strange sort of way, the "evidence" if you like, for the ethical void is how often we turn to morality to find guidance for issues (issues that affect the health, the sustainability, and the credibility of systems and structures critical to human ways of living and working – for example, government, education, religious and other institutions, etc.), that are clearly within the domain of ethics. The generation of ethics is of course the work of philosophy. The reality, the current world situation, makes clear, that when we talk ethics, we are reaching for and in need of going beyond personal ethics. What is needed to be developed are ethical principles and ethically mandated behavior for our systems, processes and institutions... and if these ethics are to be planetary in nature, that is deal with not only humanity, but life of the whole and earth itself (for example, deal with race, religion, environment, ecology, etc.), they must emanate from a philosophy that has sufficient depth, breadth, and inclusivity to be a true reflective source for the development of these ethics. What has and is emerging as the living philosophy of potential is of such a nature. At the heart of the living philosophy is something called "leading from virtue " – leading from essence - a process of leading that is emerging and accompanying this evolutionary platform shift that is, itself, struggling to come about, to unfold.

Considering and reflecting upon what is written here, we begin to form some thoughts that seem to be relevant to the educating process. We can see the encouragement and development of the ableness for being and becoming intentional – experiencing and pursuing intentionality – as a significant and real aim of education. Further we can see society's need for education to produce those who can solve the emerging problems of today being extended to encompass intentionality - intentionality in the sense that discovered "work of the heart" becomes integral to and integrated into the advancing processes and work of human society, with this work and this way of working not only enhancing the well being of human life, but all of life – the life of the whole, the life of earth itself. And certainly there is a need to develop in the young and the young at heart, the capacity and ableness to generate the planetary ethics so sorely needed at this time.

For Every Person there is a Path

Perhaps everyone at some time or other has enjoyed interacting with a lively and energetic college-bound person with the spirit and excitement having all the characteristics of one who is on a genuine quest – one who is seeking to discover and unfold their potential. Such spirited quests bring much hope and excitement, not only because it is such an important and right thing (this questioning and seeking) for young people... but especially because it is such critical work for the younger generation at this time... a time where "we the people" seem to be in a bit of a free fall – pathless.

What follows here is written to the young adult. It is not intended in any way, shape or form to be of the nature of advice, but rather written to hopefully be a useful source of reflection for anyone with a genuine quest to uncover and manifest their potential.

"My potential" lies along a path – a path of intention. It is not a goal (for example, running a four-minute mile), but rather an unfolding, perhaps like a flower unfolds to the sun. Potential is realized through intention. It requires that we have intent, an intent that requires (actually only comes about through) our being open to - receptive to - that which we are drawn to or called toward. Heartfelt listening is very important as is being aware to what is happening within me and around me when I am really "tuned in"... really working. We also get clues when we ponder and contemplate the field(s) that we harmonize with in ways that really energize us and spiritualize us. So ask yourself, "What field am I in when this sense of belonging, harmonizing, etc., occurs?" We, being creatures of life, share this characteristic with other life members. Thus we can see a cactus more readily "tuning" into a desert, than a rain forest. Examples of human life fields are automobiling, recreating, housing, clothing, etc. These are the fields upon which development and evolutionary games are played; not to be confused with technical fields such as accounting, financing, computing, engineering, etc. For technical fields to be "alive" for us, to have spirit and meaning, they need to be integrated into – that is played out on – a life field, and in truth, need to be and have a true role (rather than being a separate function) in the organization. For example, a young friend really resonated with the life field of automobiling – particularly the innovative design end. He was very skilled at computers and computer science. He actually ended up pursuing and getting a PhD in computer science – never once however losing sight of automobiling. He brought this skill (and mindset) of computer science to automobile design – where he continues to work today.

With this bit of background, we can develop a few thoughts concerning choosing a college or technical school, and generating the economics (finances) to support our choice. The choosing process – our choice – becomes more real, more conscious, and more understandable as we gain clarity of intent – or as intentionality becomes stronger. The same is true for economics. As we get clearer about our path – "our becoming" – we are more able to find, discover, attract, etc., the economic support required. There is something in the system, in our design, in how we as human beings, as human society, behave when it comes to intent – intent related to potential and becoming, that support "shows up" – not without effort of course, but in the manner of an old saying, "If there's a will, there's a way." Now, if this sounds a bit like "Have faith," that is in a real way what is being said, for faith is an integral part – a true partner, really – of pursuing and uncovering one's path – our path of potential.

Pausing for one story, a story of faith, from time to time at Anderson family gatherings, the question of how our mother (and father) found the means to raise ten children – to feed, clothe, shelter, etc. – came up. Upon occasion, we would (to borrow a popular expression of today) "do the math" and, without a doubt, prove it was not possible. We talked to our mother about this – perhaps several times – and were amazed and deeply affected by her response. For she did not describe the economics – the homemade versus store bought cost savings, the scrimping, the struggles, the real trials and tribulations. Rather she said: "Early in my life it became clear to me that God intended for family to be my work – my purpose so to speak. After that I just worked on family." In the Anderson family, we all know the beauty of "the rest of the story."

Thus the importance of and work of intent. With intent we can – relative to our education (college being an, but not the only instrument) – develop a meaningful strategy, a strategy that moves us toward and along our path. Without intent – or at least the true determination to work to see intent, to discover it – college becomes a place to go, a thing to do, a somewhat growthful experience, but it lacks instrumentality, the life-giving reality of it being an instrument to help us see and move along our path… and given the costs of college these days, economics without intent are much more difficult to gather, justify, and see as rightful and good use of family resources.

There is an old parable about the birds of the air being fed, the flowers in the field being dressed. That parable was all about faith and intent... faith that if we pursue what we are intended to be and become, the rest will fall in place.

And so, we can see...

That for every person there is a path...
> *A path to uncover...*
> *A path to wander...*
> *An unfolding way.*
A path that is along the path of the great unfolding -
> *An unforeseeable path...*
> *A knowable path...*
> *A path opened only by "yes."*
We as a people are in free fall -
> *Can't see a path...*
> *Can't see a way...*
> *Can't see an orderly procession or progression.*
Saying "yes" requires a pre-acceptance of a path...
> *Of a way -*
> *An intended way...*
> *A way of cooperating with the intended unfolding.*
An unfolding moving towards a realization of ultimate intent...
> *An unfolding not predetermined...*
> *A hazardous unfolding – even for the Source -*
> *The Source from which emanates the intent.*
An intent that mysteriously calls upon... and requires...
> *The fulfilling of roles...*
> *The carrying out of our work...*
> *Our surrendering to instrumentality.*

Stay on the Path to Becoming Human

I met an anthropologist at one time in my youth. He and I used to talk on the phone about my aspirations in life. He would say, "Well, although we possess animal natures, it seems to me the path you are looking for is the path to becoming human." "Yes," I said, "I am looking for that path. What is the path or road to becoming human?" What is the process we have to engage in while we are on the path such that we can, in a sense, realize something called humanness?

I have never given up the hope or the ideal that we can one day become fully and truly human. We see sparks of it, yet so much of our lives are spent dealing with the other aspects of ourselves (for example, our animal natures), thinking that man is all of those other phenomena. We can look at the evolution of animals and see different behaviors, and we can see those aspects in ourselves. Yet there is something called human being. Can we evolve that?

My grandmother used to sit on the porch at her home a few blocks from us. She could tell by the way I was riding my bicycle what my intention was… whether I was up to good or up to raiding a garden. Sometimes she would call me over to the porch and tell me little stories. One story she told me evolved around the theme of "You don't get off the path in one big leap." She said, "Sinning (Grandma's expression for going off the path) is a gradual process. Step off a little bit… that is okay. Then the next step, that is okay. Before you know it, you are so far off the path that you can't see the path anymore."

That is what a grandma is about; she sees you heading off the path and brings you over for a little course correction.

I think what happens to us, even though we might have good intentions, is we are attracted to something that takes us off the path. Although our intentions are good, we easily get led astray. As human beings, when we deal with issues or problems, our intent is often the right nature of intent. Yet as our work goes on, it seems like we get off the path. Why do we wander off course? We get off the path because as we engage in processes to deal with the problem, we connect up to a different philosophy than the philosophy of something called open-ended human potential. When we take our philosophy from experience or existence (from what is), it looks like we are resolving the issues, yet we are anchored in the "wrong light"... so-to-speak. Having lost the light of intention, we really cannot get where we need to go; it takes us off of the path of unfolding potential. We think things are getting better, but in reality we are not grounded in the right source – we are not grounded in the living philosophy of open-ended potential – so our work does not have in it the power or the destiny to get to higher order permanent solutions... and we stray off the path of intention.

Meditations for
Building Life Philosophy

There is a Source... an ongoing Source of creation.

There is intention and design behind the creation.

Our potential lies within the fulfilling of the intention and design.

Inherent within our human design is a longing to return to the Source of our creation, and an equally strong yearning to become... to pursue essential truths, to discover meaning, and to fulfill our life's purpose.

A living philosophy of life – a disciplined way of living and working in harmony with life processes - illuminates the path of becoming... a path in harmony with the intention of the Creator.

A living philosophy of life also seeks to see, to understand, and to honor wholeness and unity – their way of working and their way of becoming.

Thus it often finds itself to be a complementary partner with theologies that take on the work of illuminating the way of returning – the fulfilling of our longing to return to the Source of our creation.

A living philosophy readily resonates with sciences and scientific approaches that seek understanding and knowledge of the design and purpose of life's manifestations – those living sciences anchored in systemic working and wholeness.

We the people of earth were created and are intentionally designed as living creatures – creatures of life.

Life itself has purpose; and we, like other systemic members of life, also have purpose - a role in the working and ongoingness of life's processes on earth.

Fulfilling our intended role in the working and ongoingness of life, we manifest and realize our potential... and by so doing, become fully and truly human.

Life is created with open-ended potential; being members of life, we too are imbued with open-ended potential.

While life is designed to have a myriad of possibilities, true potential lies along the path of intention – the intention behind the whole of creation.

Reflection and dialogue are the means of "seeing" true potential.

The ultimate expression of true potential is realized through the spirit.

Life is not the source of spirit, but rather a means – an instrument for the manifestation of spirit – the will force of the Creator.

The spirit enters into, through, and is flavored by essence patterns – the inbuilt possibility through which the work for which life is intended is carried out.

Within each and all of life's members lies an essence – an essential pattern.

Essence patterns are the means through which the will and spirit of the Creator enter into the living and working processes of life.

Our essence – our heart of hearts – is intended and designed for the spirit to flow into and through.

Our heart's yearning to become is experienced as our essential purpose, our reason for being... our calling.

Our calling carries us beyond the restraints of who we think or imagine we are, to the freedom of who we can be and what we can become.

Community is essential to uncovering the path of our calling and realizing our potential as we pursue that path.

When we surrender to our calling – take up our work and role within the family of life on earth – spirit can be manifested.

When carried out, our essential purpose results in a spirit manifested, thus ensuring the presence of the will of the Creator in the evolutionary processes of earth and life.

Our role in the unfolding plan of the Creator extends both to and beyond the human family to include the whole of life.

Work and roles, when they operate from and bring forth essence, enable our participation in fulfilling the living purpose of humanity and its role relative to the whole of life.

A heart that has become an instrument for the working of the spirit of the Creator – a spirit manifested – is available to all of life forever... and herein lies our most true potential.

It is possible – within the scope of our design – to live and work in ways that are beyond sustaining ourselves and our lives... to live and work in ways that enable unfolding and realizing the potential of life, life's community, and life's members.

Critical to fulfilling our individual purpose and the purpose of the human family is the recognition and acceptance that we are not the source; we are intended and uniquely designed as instruments. As such, we have the inherent capacity to be subject to and cooperate with the unfolding intent of creation.

When we shift from being self-centered or human-centered to life of the whole-centered, the path of potential becomes visibly real, and the possibility of fulfilling the intent and design of our Creator much more doable.

Life on earth is ordered in, organized by, and progresses within energy fields; as living beings, we are designed and intended to harmonize and resonate with the Creator's earthly energy fields.

We can, with right "tuning" on our part, experience the virtue of a particular energy field of earth; we can gain a true and real "sense of place." This characteristic shows up in our references to people of the plains, the desert, the mountains, the tundra, and on and on.

As we tune our unique essence into a particular earthly energy field, we become working, acting, contributing parts of the ongoing working of the whole of life.

A harmonious concert of spirit emerges from the simultaneous manifesting of essences... a concert in which life's members tune themselves with the essence of their surrounding energy field.

Humankind has a role as a true working partner in sustaining the nourishing power of earth and in the realization of earth's purpose – serving as a place for life to flourish.

Our essential role and work is a particular manifestation of our essence pattern of potentiality called forth through the will of the Creator.

The process of becoming is one of being true to one's heart and staying connected to and increasingly on the path of our calling.

Our calling comes to us through our heart; it enables us to "see" how the skills, knowledge and understanding we pursue have relevance and value in fulfilling our instrumentality - our purpose.

While becoming, we strive to gain discerning capacity so that the choices we make – that which we select from the multitude of possibilities – are along the path of our potential, and intrinsically in harmony with our conscience.

While becoming, we willfully choose possibilities congruent with essence and potential, and we resist temptations of possibilities that appear and actually may be more advantageous in regards to our existence.

When we shift our efforts and attention away from hierarchical position and personal advantage toward roles that require discovery and manifestation of essence and uniqueness, life for us becomes very real... and work becomes a source of meaning and dignity in our lives.

In essence and in spirit, no one person is above another... we are in truth all equal.

Each essence is unique. These differentiations reflect the truth of our equality and are manifested (not in hierarchies, but) through roles - roles that acknowledge the realness of the work to be done, and the significance of each part played.

Rather than shy away from or build artificial protective boundaries against the processes of life, our work as humankind is to fully embrace, deeply taste, and wholeheartedly experience – through its cycles, stages, phases, agonies and ecstasies – the whole of life.

Embracing and fully experiencing the agonies and ecstasies of life, we come to know meaning and share in the awe and wonder of that which makes life real.

The source of significance is spirit. The spirit enters and flows through us as we engage in the work of discovering our purpose, taking on essential roles, and answering our calling; it is through the pursuit and acceptance of this work that spirit is manifested.

The process of deepening the understanding of our role and increasing our level of cooperation occurs through the receptivity produced by reflection and dialogue.

Reflection and dialogue produce a deeper, clearer and

more complete sense of the rightness and goodness of actions along the path on which our hearts seem to be guiding us.

Reflection and dialogue are the means by which we can prepare ourselves to hear when our hearts are being spoken to... to hear the voice of wisdom.

Through reflection and dialogue, the community gains access to ways of being and doing that were previously unimaginable... or believed to be impossible.

Through reflection and dialogue, we are given images of ways of being and doing in harmony with the Creator's intent for life – our life, life of the community, and life of the whole.

PART 6 - FACING TRUTH

Need for a Living Philosophy

Living philosophy is critical to sustaining the relevance of one's faith in the changing and evolving world. Theology and living philosophy are complementary (versus opposed) in that each works to develop, deepen, and make more whole the other. One way we can think about this is to think of theology as related to the revealed word of the Creator and living philosophy as related to the revealed works of the Creator. Theology works to deepen the understanding and meaning of the revealed truths. Living philosophy – a philosophy built through wisdom guiding reason - works to extend the understanding of the perceivable and knowable truths of the whole of creation, the works of our Creator. Humankind is so designed that we can continually extend our grasp of the working of the world – including the inner and outer workings of ourselves. This in-built capacity would seem to be a requirement if we are to consciously and conscientiously fill our given role – the work of our calling – in the processes of the world. As our understanding of the Creator's works advances, these truths increase our capacity to deepen and refine the meaning we gain from the revealed truths of the word.

A living philosophy, if it is to effectively fill its role of enabling right and good decisions in our daily living and working, needs both wisdom and reason. We can see wisdom as being associated with process. Reason, on the other hand, is more akin to structural phenomena – particularly structuring and structures. Wisdom enables us to see the whole of something and to experience the essential nature of the process that is the source of the

the whole and is also that which sustains the whole. Reason works to generate knowledge about structures and structuring – both those that exist and those that could exist. Reason is also what we call upon to generate structures. Wisdom's domain - its place of work - is the experience-able, but "invisible" process. Reason's domain is more the physical or material aspects of our reality.

For example, we can look at family - an essential process for human beings - from the perspective of process and the perspective of its structural nature. To see and experience process (the subject matter of wisdom) requires reflection. As we reflect on family process we can "see" the whole of it – the right and good working of the whole. We can begin to make considered judgments (for example, this is family; this is not family). We can "see" process as the means by which spirit enters and elevates the family. From the perspective of reason, we literally see mother, father and children. We observe how they organize who has what position, who is accountable for what, and we can discern the principles they are operating by. We also observe the structures the family has acquired or put in place to enable the processes (for example, cars, camps, houses, etc.). Wisdom is by nature a more intuitive process, whereas reason by nature is a more intellectual process. Both processes are inherent within the design of the human. Each has their particular work and significance. What is critical is that wisdom guides reason such that structuring and structures enhance process - the means of spirit and vehicle for meaning - rather than occlude it.

What is true in living philosophy as it relates to wisdom and reason is also true for theology – for once the word is revealed, our understanding and application of that is processed through the gifts of our design – through wisdom and/or reason.

A living philosophy is what enables us to live out our faith, to follow our beliefs. It is what enables us to deal with the reality of our existence and the reality of our changing, evolving world in a way that the truths of our faith can be manifested and made real in our daily living and working. For example, Christ had a living philosophy of non-violence. This enabled him to carry out and live from the truth that we all are brothers and sisters, children of a common Father – who intends that we love one another.

Humankind and life itself are at hazard when the Creator and wisdom drop out of philosophy such that reason – more specifically science – becomes the sole source of our understanding of the works. Not only does this generate incomplete understanding (for example, we tend to look at parts versus wholes) but it also disconnects us from the Creator in ways that could cause us to mistakenly treat and think of science or the scientist as if they were gods. Today we seem to be inclined in this direction; the consequences are immense. Without a true living philosophy, we cannot make right and good decisions. Without the capacity to make right and good decisions, we jeopardize all of humanity and all of life itself.

Synthesizing Faith
and Living Philosophy

We can look at the word and the works - faith and living philosophy of potential - and see a dynamic complementarity. Just for a point of reference, we could think of faith as "the collective of truths revealed through the word" – sometimes thought of as articles of faith. Faith here not only provides the basis for moral understanding, but also the vessel from which is drawn – largely through the work of reason – the articulation of theologies and theological explanation and decrees. A common central theme in this domain is the presence of good and evil and the drama that has historically existed through the contest and struggle for power between the two... a theme that both lifts up and lends itself to notions of human weakness and failings... and an ongoing personal struggle with this duo... a struggle that includes effort toward soul perfecting and establishing a "good" relationship – personal and societal – with our Creator. This struggle is both fueled by and critical to our successfully fulfilling our longing to return: to return home, to be at one with the Source – our Creator.

The collectives of truths – articles of faith and anchors of the living philosophy of potential – begin to emerge as expressions of people... people of faith, people of intentionality. We can see the longing to return and the yearning to become as distinctive, but complementary aspects of one people – two aspects of our design. This imagery holds much hope, hope that has its origin in the truth of our oneness – we all emanate from a Common Source – and the truth that love is present to both sides of our design. On the faith side we are clear about the necessity to love our Creator and to love one another; on the intentionality side we understand that if love is not present in the process, it will not be present in the outcomes. And too, the potential for synthesis – the means for bringing about wholeness – is now visibly present. We understand that differentiation must occur before synthesis can take place – a differentiation at the level of essence. Essence is emerging; the reality, the equality, the necessity, the complementarity of the intentional side is establishing its presence. More and more we can witness the stirring of this truth. The realization that we are part of life – by intention and design – is growing. We are increasingly not so much separate from life and our living earth, but seeing ourselves within the whole of it. This awakening, especially as it becomes more active, more visible, and more understood, will in truth not threaten faith, but rather serve to enliven it - to repotentialize and to respiritualize faith - and in this way we can more fully live out the truth of our oneness... and through the work of synthesis begin to bring about a true and real sense of wholeness... a oneness and wholeness... a significant step along the path of becoming fully and truly human.

Gaining Clarity of Wholeness

A recent article in our local newspaper regarding Katharine Jefferts Schori being elected to lead the U. S. Episcopal Church is the source point of these reflections. This newspaper article included several quotes related to her personal theological understandings which I found to be openly refreshing, most encouraging, and real sources of hope. I learned that she too has come to regard transparency as essential to integrity, and, I might add, to our progressing in our humanness. One particular quote was, for me, not only an exciting source of hope, but also the source of reflective thoughts that will unfold in this writing. It went on to say that Jefferts Schori personally believes in a relationship with God through Jesus, but does not see it as the only path. This was followed by a quote, "If we insist we know the one way to God, we're putting God in a very small box." There is much hope in this notion... hope in that it opens up a pathway for reconciliation – true reconciliation – that can bring about wholeness... a wholeness that recognizes the truth of our oneness. Blind imposition, like blind obedience, does not lead to wholeness, the wholeness that humanity - individually and systemically - is intended to struggle for and realize.

This comment and quote brought to mind a similar or related notion expressed several years ago by Pope John Paul II. The occasion of his bringing forth this "path to salvation" notion was his speaking to a very large gathering of young adults – most of whom, if not all, as I recall, were of the Islamic faith. Through the magic of television, I was able to be at this interaction. His message was both simple and powerful. Essentially, from memory, what he said was this:

Pope:	Can we agree there is but one God?
Youth:	Yes!
Pope:	Can we agree that we will reject any ideology based on violence and hate?
Youth:	Yes! We can agree to that.
Pope:	Can we agree to follow only those ideologies based on peace and love?
Youth:	Yes! We can agree to that.
Pope:	I believe that if you enter upon the path of peace and love, you will meet and come to know Christ. When it comes to peace and love, Christ is the exemplar – the perfect model.

This, I experienced as an authentic and genuine expression and manifestation of faith – true faith, pure faith, faith empty of the need to impose... empty of the need to have power over.

It is this notion of path – path to God/ path to salvation – expressed by both Bishop Schori and Pope John Paul II that has provided an energizing source for my own reflection and contemplation. My work, while it is not theological, does have a clear sense of path – a philosophical path of potential... a path toward fulfilling the intent and design of the Creator. In some ways it could be thought of as a path from the Creator, a path where the work is to enable the intended unfolding – the unfolding of enfolded potential... a way of participating in and fulfilling our role in the ongoing creation. The understanding of this path has been a lifelong pursuit of mine. And now as I stand firmly in the seventh decade of my life, I can see clearly the complementarity of the two paths – the path to God and the path of our potential - and the requirement of a harmonious relatedness to be established for wholeness to be realized.

The notions of oneness and wholeness have had an ongoing presence along this path of my life and my work. Clarity in regards to oneness seemed to arrive earlier than (precede) my current understanding of wholeness. For me at least, the sense of oneness – oneness as a people, oneness with the universe – came about quite readily through reflection and contemplation. The truth of our oneness – one people, one earth – was not only clear through reflecting on the works of the Creator, but equally clear through the teachings of Christ – particularly through his words as he responded to the request to teach us to pray: Our Father... our Common Father, of whom we are all children, children of the one and the same God. Yet, as we well know, the acceptance of this truth – of living it out – still provides for us a bit of a struggle.

Wholeness, on the other hand, has taken greater effort to gain some clarity of, which is strange in a way, because from early on, particularly as a teenager and young adult, the notion of wholeness was a source of discord in my life - a discord that continued and continues today. Now, however, I have come to understand that this discord, at essence, has as its source two urges – our longing to return to the Ultimate Source, and our yearning to become. This becoming – the discovery of purpose, our reason for being, our work, our calling – has been present as an urge, but not really addressable because of the absence of philosophy – the absence of a practical, practice-able, living philosophy; a void that, if it continues to exist, not only has severe consequences to us personally, but one that hinders, if not halts our ability to advance our humanness.

What has now become clear - if oneness and whole-ness, two truths of our existence, truths of the intent and design of our Creator, are to become real for us – is that a synthesis of the path to salvation (the path of returning to the Source) and the path of potential (the path of our becoming fully and truly human) must occur. There is much hope in the willingness to go back to essence – to take issues to essence... to see essential truths and right and good working of the whole within which issues exist... or to which issues relate. By so doing, wisdom and wise choices become possible... and of course this way of working makes increasingly possible the bringing about of a harmonious relatedness between the path to God and the path of our work on earth, the path of ful-filling the intent and design of the Creator.

In my recent reflections, I have begun to see some images and relationships between those images that I have not seen previously (in other reflections and con-templations). While some of the elements were present, the relatedness, relationships and clarity were not previ-ously there. These images are from and for intuition – the intuition of wholeness. As such they are not mechan-ical or scientific models, but rather envisionings having more the character of truth - intended to be reflected upon, and contemplated in order to see and gain increased depth and understanding. A bit of orientation may help us gain more value from these images.

First off, it is helpful to recall that the perspective we hold ultimately determines the life path we take, our thinking and behavior along that path, and therefore the way we live and work. A second and helpful orientation is that these images have emerged from a life of the whole perspective. Another reference point is a notion that is present within the living philosophy of potential.

As we look out into creation – the world we exist in – we can notice several related but distinctive phenomena. We can with our senses (often aided by instruments) perceive and observe a material, physical, energetic aspect or plane of our existence. Behind the material plane of our existence we can (aided by reflection) experience essence – the essence of a forest, the essence of a child - an essence character or pattern out from which emerges the particular structures and behaviors that we see… a plane of essence that is as equally real, if less visible, as the physical plane. Reflecting further upon our existence we can see a third plane – a plane beyond the planes of material and essence – a plane of spirit, spirit which seems to be behind or super-ordinate to essence and therefore to material. A simple depiction allows us to maintain a working image for further thought and reference.

With this orientation in place, we can move to an imagery that both emerges from and speaks to intuition. The aim here is not to provide a definitive answer, but rather depict that which, through reflection, contemplation and dialogue, can be deepened and evolved.

SPIRIT
Deep within, in the innermost aspects of our humanness, is an urge, an urge we experience both as a longing to return to the Source and a yearning to become. This urge is one that emanates from the truth of our oneness, and our struggle to achieve intended wholeness – individually and as a people - an urge that is both a source of spirit and a manifestation of spirit. The longing

to return is often viewed in terms of a soul – a soul returning to its Source – a process of salvation, of being saved... of going home to God. The yearning to become is more experienced as striving to be and become what we are intended to be – to discover and fulfill our purpose... to fulfill the intent and design of our Creator. And while returning often leans toward the individual – a personal relationship with God, my salvation – becoming, especially through time, leans toward the larger whole of which we are a part – the whole of humanity, the whole of life.

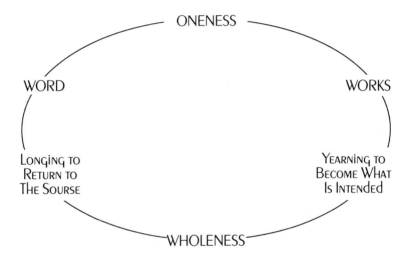

ESSENCE

Humankind has, at essence, two sources of revelation: revelation through the word that emanates from that aspect of the Source we often call God, and revelation through the manifested works of that aspect of the Source we often call the Creator. God and the Creator are one and the same Source. Yet two paths, distinct, but obviously not independent of each other (and truly representing two realities of our humanness), emanate from and lead to the one and the same Source. Both paths, if we are to take them up – to walk along them in an authentic and genuine way – require faith, faith that holds the experiential character of surrendering – surrendering, in one sort of way, one's will for faith; on the one hand – on the path of returning - faith in a just and loving God, and on the other hand – on the path of becoming - faith in the intent and design of the Creator. Each path also has a central core of essential truths, often thought of as articles of faith on the word side, and anchors of the living philosophy of potential on the works side. Both the word and the works sides have within them, essential work – real work of understanding morality and developing ethics – that is ongoing... ongoing work because earth, life on earth, and the universe for that matter, are not stagnant, but rather dramatic, dynamic, unfolding phenomena. Thus, while there may be times when we experience "quiet periods," there is often before us an emerging reality that calls upon us to deepen our understanding of morality – what it now means to be moral - and to further develop our ethics – in what context must we now be ethical. Currently we (humankind) are experiencing a context shift from being human-centered to being life of the whole-centered. Being moral and ethical are the primary means for perfecting and advancing our humanness. The essential work of both of these does not call for the discarding of previous essential truths, but rather a renewed engagement of these truths, and at certain times a return to - a seeking of - the essence of the truths themselves. The emerging reality of today seems to be such a time.

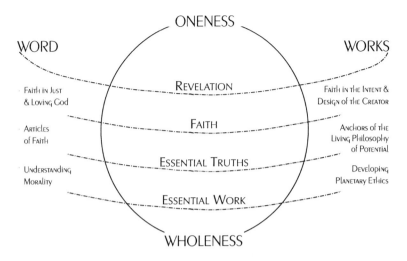

ONENESS

WORD   WORKS

Faith in Just   REVELATION   Faith in the Intent &
& Loving God   Design of the Creator

Articles   FAITH   Anchors of the
of Faith   Living Philosophy
                                                     of Potential

Understanding   ESSENTIAL TRUTHS   Developing
Morality   Planetary Ethics

                            ESSENTIAL WORK

WHOLENESS

MATERIAL

Now we have moved into the realm of concreteness – the working home of reason – a place where wisdom can go unnoticed or perhaps be forgotten... a place where we can readily see the working of perspective. Here we can quickly connect to many of the issues of today, issues between religions, between religion and science, etc., issues that are the source of discord and often divisiveness, issues that naturally – almost automatically – bring forth the perspective of problem – problems to solve, wrongs to right, issues to fix. We can however, willfully choose a different perspective – a perspective of potential – and in this way we see that which we need to bring into being... a perspective of potential whereby we take all issues to essence, and remembering that spirit enters into material through essence, begin to work to respiritualize all processes – the essential processes of life and the processes of returning and becoming as well. This is the work at hand – that which needs to unfold. There is no doubt this work will call upon and demand faith – true faith - for as I can see so clearly, it really is only and all about faith: faith in a just and loving God, faith in the intent and design of the Creator.

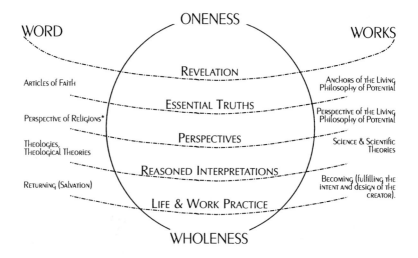

WORD

ONENESS

WORKS

REVELATION

Articles of Faith

Anchors of the Living
Philosophy of Potential

ESSENTIAL TRUTHS

Perspective of Religions*

Perspective of the Living
Philosophy of Potential

PERSPECTIVES

Theologies,
Theological Theories

Science & Scientific
Theories

REASONED INTERPRETATIONS

Returning (Salvation)

Becoming (fulfilling the
intent and design of the
creator).

LIFE & WORK PRACTICE

WHOLENESS

* *Christian, Islamic, Jewish, Native American, etc.*

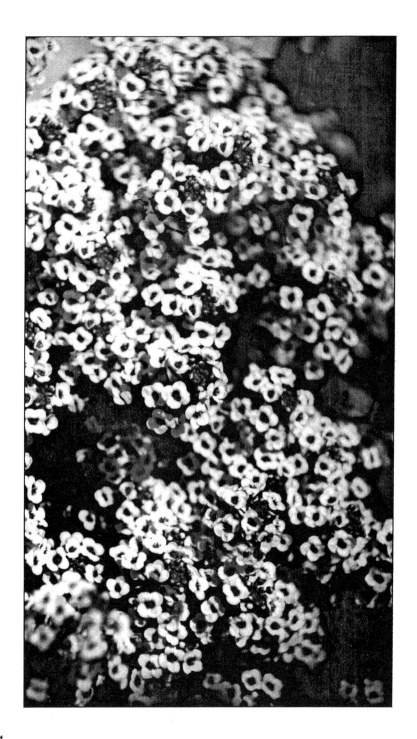

Reflecting on the Essence of Who We Are and What We Are Intended to Be and Become

To begin: there is a Common Source for the whole of creation... a Creative Force from and through which the whole of the universe emanates... a Source and Force that lies beyond that which is perceivable through the senses. The essential nature of the Ultimate Source is love. A characteristic of the Source is intentionality. This intentionality is revealed to humankind through the word and the works - the whole of the universe, the totality of creation.

We, humankind, are particular manifestations of the works of our Creator. We have been imbued with the characteristic of life – we are living human beings. As such, we are not only members of the human family, but we are also real and true members of the larger community of life. Humankind is not separate from, above or outside of the larger whole of life... a truth that does not diminish the uniqueness of our design, but rather increases the significance of the roles we have been given and are called upon to play.

At the essential core of our design are two impulses or urges: the longing to return, and the yearning to become. Built within each and all is the longing to return to the Source of our creation, and a yearning to become what we are intended to be – a yearning to discover and fulfill our purpose, our calling. Whereas these innermost strivings can be ignored, denied or occluded by the forces of culture and religion and the demands of existence, they are – through reflection – accessible and experience-able. This is particularly true of the becoming aspect of ourselves in the time we are now living.

We human beings have a characteristic way of working that involves structures and structuring. We have a desire and requirement (that seems to exceed that of other living creatures) to generate and produce both visible and invisible structures - structures that emanate from function and form, doing and being, science/engineering and art. We also create mental structures around phenomena so that we can reflect on, analyze and think about them.

Two phenomena that we have and continue to work to build mental constructs around are the word and the works of our Creator. Through reflection and study, we seek to gain increased clarity and deeper understanding of the intent and design of the Creator; and by so doing, we gain truer insight as to who and why we are... as well as, perhaps having the Creator himself revealed to us. The common name for our mental constructs around the word is religion; and that name we attach to our constructs around the works is philosophy.

Religion relates to that innermost aspect of our humanness: the longing to return to and be one with the Source of our creation... a longing that seems to be shared by the Creator. Religion falls in the domain or sphere of the human family and its relationship to the Creator. As such, it takes on the character of human-centeredness.

Philosophy – living philosophy – relates to that other innermost aspect of our humanness: the yearning to become. Whereas religion has as its aim the hereafter, living philosophy holds the here and unfolding now as its aim. It works to enable the seeing of our role – individually and collectively - not only in relationship to human life, but also relative to the whole of life and the life processes of earth.

Living philosophy is life of the whole-centered. Life-centeredness does not diminish humankind or human life, but rather adds significance to the part we are intended to play in the unfolding plan of the Creator... a part that carries with it the requirement that as we engage in our natural tendency to improve our existence - advance humankind and human life - we do so under the wisdom and guidance of what is right and good for the whole of life... for life itself.

Living philosophy, like its complementary partner, religion, recognizes the one Source of creation. It works to access the wisdom behind the works such that reason can be properly guided as it goes about generating structures. Living philosophy guides the mind that ponders the structure and structuring of the universe to look for understanding that will enable all human beings to become better instruments, better role players, and better enablers of the evolutionary and unfolding intent of the Creator. Living philosophy demands that humankind give full consideration to the life processes of earth and the whole of life by accessing our conscience and allowing it to guide us as we go about the business of living and working. It requires that we not only ask, "Is this right and good for humanity?" but also, "Is it equally right and good for life itself?"

Our ability to access and act from our conscience is dependent upon our capacity to see and honor essence... for it is through essence that we are able to be true and faithful to the intent and design of our Creator. Whether we are dealing with a physical thing, a living being, a living system, or a planetary energy field, the intent and the wisdom behind its creation lies in its essence – the source of patterns that represent its true nature and work in the world. This essential understanding is revealed to us through reflection... reflection that works to see the essence and whole of something, and carries with it the intent to be an instrument, thus denying the illusion of being the actual source. Reflecting in this way, wisdom is accessed, spirit can enter, and processes unfold beyond that which could be created by other means.

Living philosophy has faith in the intent and design of the Creator. It acknowledges a Source of creation, and readily accepts our instrumentality - the need for humankind to uncover and cooperate with the intent and design of the Creator. It acknowledges the reality of the unfolding intent of the Creator as being one of directed uncertainty... not predetermined, but one in which humankind has a significant and critical role to play - a role that, given the precarious situation facing life on earth (human life, the whole of life), requires we work expeditiously and diligently to realize the potential that lies within our design. We need, and life needs us, to become fully and truly human – to pursue a path along which the potential of each and all can be realized.

A Seeing of Truth

I became aware of being in a vision... a holographic or three-dimensional vision. It was like being in a bubble and all were in the bubble... we all were there together.

I was standing next to this personage who had the being of Christ. All of my discernment said that Christ was who was there. We were standing there with two scenes in front of us – one to the left and one to the right. He was standing with one foot in each of these images.

It was a totally silent image. This personage and I were standing side-by-side. Words did not feel necessary. The envisioning and the experiencing of the presence began to work innerly... as expressed thoughts. His hands were out, and what was before us was obvious. I had an overwhelming sense of togetherness. Then the words became present, but not with sound. I am saying this in a sequential manner; yet it did not happen sequentially, but all at once. I am describing what was heard, seen and experienced, without interpretation.

The left-hand scene was clear imagery. It was people standing with rocks in their hands, and a woman cowering in the corner against the wall. The right-hand scene was a very fuzzy mirror image of the scene on the left. We could see the shapes and forms, but the faces were fuzzy... in a sense, I could not tell if they were being created or erased. I almost felt that if I could turn on the light, then maybe I would be able to see it more clearly. That is when the image of "becoming" showed itself in the scene on the right. The personage of Christ put his right hand over and I then had the sense this side is "becoming," while the left-hand side is all "salvation."

Then the "becoming side" words were spoken, "If love is not present in the process, it will not be present in the outcome." The mirror image of those words on the "salvation" side were "Let he among you who is without sin cast the first stone." The words of love – the words of becoming - were in the same voice – Christ's voice – and were the mirror of the words of salvation.

Stone silence... I could "see" the words. They were being written. The words in each side were on a plank... it was the conscience plank. The words were so clear... there was no confusion in the words.

While those faces and shapes of humans on the right side were fuzzy, I could see they were single persons and groups – any person or group we find ourselves personifying as the enemy in order to achieve our goals. These fuzzy people standing around all had rocks in their hands. They personified any group that you have to motivate to pick up the rock to stone the perceived enemy. There were environmentalists, politicians, rights and peace activists, government, business and religious leaders, and on and on and on. At any time, anyone could be throwing and anyone could be thrown at. That is what made "If love is not in the process, it will not be in the outcome" the mirror of "Whoever is without sin, throw the first rock."

As his arm opened and reached out to the left, Christ said, "This is what was unfolding then," and to the right, "and this is what is unfolding now."

All of this began to be drawn into me, outerly disappearing... then innerly, these words came: "Life, liberty and the pursuit of dignity." Then came "experience the fullness and wholeness of life... that is what America is for - a place for that." Then, "liberty – the freedom to choose the process by which I develop my soul, realize my potential, and surrender to my instrumentality." Then the words were, "pursuit of dignity - become fully and truly human in the dignified image that was intended." As the bubble – all of both images and Christ – started being absorbed into me, these thoughts were unfolding and the inner experience was that of joyous nervousness. I was experiencing the doubtless realness of what was occurring as I stood there outside the morning shower.

There was no pre-thought before the vision came. It was just there... and it coalesced all.

PART 7 · Being Clear

THAT WAS THEN;
NOW IS NOW

In the beginning,
  our very first act of disobedience
    was to interfere with the intended working of the world...

In the beginning, at the earliest of human times... through the intentional act of the Creator... there emerged from the earth, a people – a living people of earth. The people enjoyed an unending abundance, constant happiness, and real peace. A harmony existed among all the creatures of earth.

At the start of the beginning, the intention of the Creator was made known. The Creator put forth instructions or laws by which the people were to live in community. Now the people, being unique among life's creatures, could choose to obey or not to obey the Creator's laws. The people, by design, were endowed with free will – and as such were not subject to the automatic behavior and obedience practiced by the other creatures of earth. Somewhere along the way, temptation became ever more present. Succumbing to this temptation, the people chose to act from themselves, rather than live in accord with the Creator's instructions.

The people became increasingly knowledgeable, but decreasingly wise. More and more they used their knowledge to serve themselves; less and less regard did they have for the Creator's intention. As time passed - as they progressed along their chosen path – the people began to experience illness, sorrow, war, strife, woe and emptiness... the opposite of the beginning. Earth, the very home of life itself, became threatened.

That was then...

Now is now.

The past is past... the future is yet to unfold. Now is the time to uncover a new path – a new way of being.

The people are beginning to awaken.
Conscience is being stirred to life.
Love is seeking to enter.
Hearts are opening themselves to wisdom.
Intuition is coming into play.

There is a growing sense of a calling...
    A call to reclaim our heritage...
        our heritage of peace and wholeness...
A call to fulfill our role.

An ethic is striving to emerge...
An ethic for living wisely on this earth...
An ethic born from essential truths...
    ... the truth of our being a people of earth.
    ... the truth of our shared humanness.
    ... the truth of our being members of the commu-
        nity of life.
    ... the truth of our Common Source.
    ... the truth of our calling to become fully and
        truly human.
    ... the truth that all are called, and each may
        choose.

Moving Towards Wholeness

Commonly recognized is the real void of ethics and ethical practices in our institutions, organizations and culture... in our ways of living and working. Less recognized is the urgent need for a living philosophy – one that we can live out and from. For it is the work of philosophy to provide the thought base for the generation of ethics. A living philosophy is a people's philosophy, one that is appropriate for the dynamics of today, and one that moves us upward... in the direction of rightness and goodness... towards wholeness.

The aim of the living philosophy of potential is to generate the thought base and process for developing the wholistic ethics needed today. The living philosophy of potential is unique in that it comes from a life of the whole perspective – a perspective of and for wholeness... a perspective that seeks to see and understand the work required for moving towards wholeness. Moving towards wholeness and away from that which divides is a necessary direction for ourselves, our country and beyond.

With a life of the whole perspective we can go about the work of developing planetary ethics – the nature of ethics needed for today's world, not only to serve the whole of humankind, but the whole of life as well.

A life of the whole perspective allows us to pursue the work of enabling run up versus being confined solely to the work of arresting run down. Reflecting on the working of the whole enables us to gain access to the wisdom required for making wise choices, the making of wise choices being greatly benefited by an understanding of the two types of work.

Imaging the work of arresting run down, we begin to picture some critical elements, and see their relationship as a set. We see for instance that this work tends to anchor itself in existence. It acknowledges that that which comes into existence tends to run down, thus the effort to arrest run down. For example, roads need repairing, houses require maintenance, water and air need to be cleaned of pollutants, etc. Arresting run down calls upon intellect and reason, follows a problem-solving path, and looks to analysis, segmentation, facts and proof, all of which commonly lead to a focus on a part, and therefore to partial solutions.

Imaging the work of enabling run up, we also begin to see some of its elements and patterns. Here we, of necessity, work to see systemic relatedness, how each element systemically relates to the others, and how its work and role affects the working of all others and of the whole... a working relatedness that the statement, "If you touch one, you touch them all," helps us to keep in mind. Envisioning the whole, its right and good working, and the systems and systemic relatedness within become primary. Here the anchor is essence rather than existence; potential versus problem becomes the orientation and approach; intuition – the intuition of wholeness – is called upon; and the seeking of wisdom, developing wise choices, and wisdom guiding reason come to the fore. At this time, in the dramatic reality of today, a further demand is placed upon the work of enabling run up, that being the demand to shift – to shift as a people, a people of earth – from being human-centered to being life of the whole-centered. In the absence of a life of the whole perspective, we cannot carry out the nature of run up work required... the work that is absolutely necessary, not only for humanity, but for life itself.

Now, to be clear, there has always been the presence and need for both types of work – arresting run down and enabling run up – and there exists within each a real possibility for developmental processes and developmental work. Commonly at issue is the question of balance, and perhaps today the issue is the need for shifting the imbalance – that is, not shifting from being heavily weighted towards arresting run down to some middle point, but rather shifting to being heavily weighted in the direction of enabling the work of run up. This emphasis towards enabling run up seems to be valid not only for actions, but also for that from which we take our direction: that which leads our thinking surely must be anchored in a life of the whole perspective, regardless of the type of work in which we are engaged.

Given the aim of our work – *moving towards wholeness and away from that which divides* – with a bit of reflection, it becomes quite obvious that clearly we cannot legislate wholeness... thus this is truly a grassroots process. Curiously enough, seeing and embracing wholeness demands that love be present in the process. Love is the orientation and energization of heart and mind required to truly experience and see wholeness. *If love is not present in our process, love will not be present in the outcome.*

Coming from Emotion

At this time, on this earth, there is an unfolding urge – an intuitively obvious need – to *move towards wholeness and away from that which divides*. The realization of this urge calls for a particular type of work, the work of enabling run up. The taking on and carrying out of this work requires intuition – the intuition of wholeness – and reflection, reflective dialogue, and the taking on of roles related to the work of our heart - our calling, the path of our passion - all of which need to emanate from a life of the whole perspective.

The passion related to enabling run up is anchored in essence, intention and intentional working. This passion is of a different nature than the strong feelings we often experience in relationship to the work of arresting run down. The passion of enabling run up, the passion of our calling, a true emotion, emotes from and through essence – the core of intentionality.

The strong feelings we have related to arresting run down, often experienced and described by others as our being passionate about something, anchor themselves in existence – something is occurring "out there" that evokes strong feelings within us. These feelings often energize us to take up a cause, right wrongs, fix what is wrong, etc. ...efforts that have the character or pattern of arresting run down, the elimination of interference with the achievement of goals, etc., all of which relate to existence.

Now enabling the work of run up and arresting run down work are true companions, realities of life that serve different purposes. One deals more with an act of creation – bringing something into being – and the other more deals with the truth that that which comes into existence tends to run down. In a similar sort of way, emotions and feelings are related realities of life. They too have different anchor points, different sources. Emotion connects to essence; feelings connect to existence. However, with a bit of reflection and intuitive processing, we can see that while feelings can be both positive and negative, there are, in reality, no negative emotions. For example, love – pure love – is a positive force.

However, feelings, be they positive or negative, particularly those that just "show up," or are spontaneously evoked by something we witness, hear or see, can be a useful source of reflection for gaining clarity in regards to essence, the work of our heart, our calling. Often there lies behind the feeling, a pattern or connection that, through reflection and reflective processing, can provide some insight to our calling, our work of the heart. And too, negative energy, can be an energizing source towards the positive.

And so, as we pursue the work of enabling run up, it seems important that we gain a clear notion, that we clearly differentiate the passion of our path from that which we are commonly passionate about.

Understanding the Work and Working of Ethics

Developing planetary ethics is the reflective work... the "called for" work... the grassroots work... of today's generation. In one sort of way, we could describe ethics as the behavioral guidelines - principles and rules - which we willfully impose upon ourselves, or consciously accept as real requirements of particular roles that we take on – especially roles that involve systems or institutions that are critical to the healthy and intentional working of our society. At times we experience ethics as an inner talking preceding an action – an action which, if we listen carefully, we know in our heart of hearts as to whether or not it is a right and good - right for the one, good for the whole - thing to do... or at the very least, harmless to the whole and others. Besides the inner talking, there is the experience and process of the community speaking – at times to itself, but frequently to those in essential roles in systems and institutions critical to the well being of society (e. g., education, religion, business, government, recreation, entertainment, press, etc.). We notice this "community speaking" most often in regard to what is commonly thought of as scandalous behavior, a "speaking" that often takes the form of outrage, expectations of corrective actions – consequences - by those in charge, and increasingly legal action, especially when the community perceives inadequate or inappropriate corrective action by the "powers that be." This "community speak" seems to take its strength and its sense of obligation and responsibility from the reality that in America, power goes from the people to its institutions – not only our governing institutions, but the critical institutions of society as well. The community, recognizing the absolute necessity for having trust and confidence in the working, decision making, and actions of these institutions, turns to ethics - the higher plane, that which is above the law - to ensure right and good management of these institutions.

Now a curious thing has been happening of late. There is a tendency to start our thinking from the perspective of legality. Thus perhaps we automatically think "legal action," when scandalous behavior occurs. There also is a tendency to lump all "scandalous behavior" into the category of morals or morality. The effect of both of these is that ethics, ethicality, and ethical behavior are in a real sort of way disappearing from our consciousness, and therefore from our conscientiousness. The ethical vigilance required to sustain the vitality, vigor and viability of our society, is relatively inactive – "off the screen" of our everyday life so to speak. Yet we know, intuitively obvious is the truth, that the destiny of an unethical society is disorder, collapse and ruin...

Now to sort out the contrasting difference and work of morals and ethics is beyond the scope of this reflection, but perhaps a few comments that emerged from a recent conversation with a friend would be helpful. Stated most simply, morals are between you and your Maker. Ethics are between you, me and the community. Moral infractions carry with them the possibility of forgiveness, a forgiveness that calls for genuine sorrow and contriteness, with the ultimate judgment in the hands of your Maker. Ethical infractions, from an American perspective, carry with them the possibility of restoring the peoples' trust and confidence in the perpetrator and institutions, a possibility (at least for the institutions) that has to be realized if we are to sustain an intentionally working society; thus exists the requirement for overtness, clarity of corrective action, and the necessity for consequences, up to and including removal from the role. We can see from an intentionally working society standpoint, "moral forgiveness" in and of itself is inadequate for those which are truly "ethical infractions" - those infractions which violate the trust and confidence so necessary to sustaining our critical institutions.

We are being called upon to add to our experience and understanding of societal ethics, the planet and mother earth, and so the conversation has to shift. Now the "inner talking" and "community speaking" need to include the voice of earth herself… hearing and heeding her cries.

Ethical Guidelines for Ourselves as People of Earth

One of the truths we have come to understand is that if love is not present in the process, it will not be present in the outcome.

If the ethics we generate, on any subject and for any process, are to encompass the whole of life - the whole of our living humanness - love must be present in the process. With love and through love it is possible to have and to hold as a serious intent this common aim for all ethical guidelines:

To advance humanness... to enrich life –
the life of the whole, and the whole of life on this earth.

Reflecting on the "absence" of love we can see a possibility of enhancing existence – at least materially – but not of having access to the spirit and meaning that love brings.

Reflecting further we comfortably see that it is natural to want to move up planes of existence - to have a better life for ourselves, for our children, and for future generations. Love entering through the eye of the heart does not seek to deny or diminish this natural inclination seemingly inherent within us; rather love works to illuminate the truth and wisdom that would enable – that would let us see – ways of making progress that would advance our humanness, and would increasingly honor and harmonize with the whole of life.

With love in our process and holding in our hearts the

common aim, "to advance humanness... to enrich life – the life of the whole, and the whole of life on this earth," the eye of the heart, reflecting on these five ethical guidelines, would seek to see their essentiality, wisdom, wholeness and systemic relatedness:

- No occlusion to the "tuning" of the planetary life energy field.
- On entering a territory, seek to understand and honor, rather than interfere with, the spiritual culture and other essential life processes.
- Honor and understand the working of the life of the whole.
- Pursue technology and approaches that enable community self determination and environmental amelioration.
- Create processes that engender understanding and discourage divisiveness.

Ethical Guideline One

"No occlusion to the "tuning" of the planetary life energy field."

As we reflect on our experiencing - innerly experiencing - the planetary life energy fields of earth, we can with a bit of effort recreate – in the eye of our heart – the depth, the nature, and the significance of our tuning experience. We notice that as living human beings we can innerly organize ourselves in ways that we become truly receptive to that which is at work here. We can tune ourselves into the spirit and energy of the landscape before us... and more impressively this effort of ours brings about – within us – a tuning by the life energy field itself. The life energy field truly works on us, a phenomenon recognized by the statements, "You go to the mountains to build your mind; you go to the ocean to soothe your soul."

Reflection on our experience of tuning into and being tuned by life energy fields leads to the understanding of the necessity for being-to-being interactions. Such interactions are not only energizing, but through patient receptivity on our part, bring about an access and elevation of spirit that itself leads to a coalescence – a oneness, a wholeness – not only within oneself, but with the whole of the universe. There is a deep sense of connectedness, at times a diminishment of self, that leads to a true appreciation – an overwhelming sense of awe and wonder - and in that moment we gain a taste of what it means to be fully alive – to be fully present to our living human nature.

Whatever is at work as we tune into and are tuned by life energy fields is undoubtedly significant, and obviously an intended aspect of our design… and whereas we may be the highest order form of life on earth, we can readily witness and observe the tuning capacity of our fellow creatures of life – the flora and fauna of the life energy field. It too is not only an aspect of their design – their living nature – but an inherent process in the working of life itself, a process that produces a particularized living system relative to that planetary life energy field… a living system that is both produced and enhanced – in both vitality and viability – by particular structures.

Now we know from experience, that there are times when it is difficult, if not impossible, to innerly organize ourselves such that we can be receptive to tuning. Preoccupation of mind, hurriedness, inattentiveness, etc., all work to interfere with our tuning capacity.

Likewise, what works innerly also works outerly. Structures and structuring can be present that interfere with our ability to tune into and be tuned by the life energy field. What is true for us is likely true for all of life's creatures.

Finally we understand that we are people of earth - people who live within and occupy particular life energy fields. Tuning into and being tuned by a life energy field gives us access to the virtue and spirit of the field itself... a process that, we are beginning to see and understand, enables us to come together in ways previously not attainable.*

Ethical Guideline Two

"ON ENTERING A TERRITORY, SEEK TO UNDERSTAND AND HONOR, RATHER THAN INTERFERE WITH, THE SPIRITUAL CULTURE AND OTHER ESSENTIAL LIFE PROCESSES."

Life's way is process... process that becomes more visible, more embraceable, through ebb and flow, cycles, cyclical patterns, and patterns within cycles. Culture is a process, a life process, an essential life process. It is the way of the people – the people's way of living, way of working, way of worshipping, honoring, dignifying, celebrating, etc. Culture, when it is truly working, is in reality a living being. As such, it experiences all that is true for life. It struggles to survive, to sustain itself, to develop, to evolve... it struggles to become.

Behind the visible manifestations of life lies the life force

*See "Becoming; Right for the Heart... Good for the Whole," Path of Potential, 2005, for understanding of what becomes possible when a community adopts the virtue of the land as their living philosophy.

– that which continues to bring life into existence, and works to sustain life's course along the intended unfolding path. Once again, culture, like life, has that which lies behind its visible and embraceable elements - the systemic elements of values, rituals, totems, language, taboos, etc. Behind these visible elements of culture lies its essence, its virtue, its spirit – the particular manifestation of will entangled with love.

It is the active presence and manifestation of essence, virtue and spirit that are the ongoing source of what we have come to see as the spiritual culture of the people. Spiritual culture is the means by which the people can be and become that which they truly are... their way of being authentic throughout their journey. It is the way they stay connected to the Source of creation, their means of participating in the great unfolding, of taking on and fulfilling purposes... purposes that serve the whole of humanity, that work to advance our humanness along the intended path, and ultimately serve the whole of life. As such, interference, be it intentionally or unthinkingly caused, has consequences of significance to each and all – to each of humanity, and to all of life.

Ethical Guideline Three

"Honor and understand the working of the life of the whole."

Life is about wholes; life always operates within and relative to particular wholes. These living wholes work to sustain their integrity by willfully sustaining their connection to their essence, their virtue, and their life purpose. It is within wholes that individuality is meaningfully manifested, and significance is realized.

Wholes provide for life a sort of boundedness, not a boundedness that would create a closed nature, but rather the nature of boundedness that brings about the orderliness and organizing necessary to carry out the intended work – the essential work, the purposeful work - of life within a particular whole. In the absence of the presence of such wholes, life cannot go about its work; life flounders, and access to the life force diminishes.

Seeking to honor the working of the life of the whole brings to the fore the notion of sustaining integrity - the necessity to ensure the actions taken do not violate or disenable wholeness and the capacity to bring about the orderliness and organizing required for life to carry out its work. This capacity has a component – a requirement – related to scale. Sufficient scale must be present to carry out the particular life's work. A rain forest in our back yard, for example, would not be of sufficient scale to carry out the life work of the rain forest.

A second consideration in regards to honoring the working of the life of the whole relates to structures and structuring. There are structures that can naturally integrate into the working of the processes of life, and there are those that cannot. For those that cannot, we either need to refrain from creating or using them, or we need to generate methodologies whereby they are prevented from entering into the working of life's processes. And in reality, even for those that can integrate naturally, there is most often, if not always, a need for thoughtful methodologies. With a bit of reflection we can see both the necessity for and the benefit of understanding the structuring that comes about as a result of the structures we create and introduce into living systems.

Honoring the working of the life of the whole also

demands that we see and acknowledge the systemic nature of that which occurs within living wholes. Acting in accord with the reality that each element is related to and affects the working of the others is an inescapable requirement of honoring. "Touch one, you touch them all," may be a useful phrase to remind us – to awaken us – to the necessity of honoring the working of the life of the whole, and of the consequences should we willfully or unknowingly choose to disregard it.

Ethical Guideline Four

> "PURSUE TECHNOLOGY AND APPROACHES THAT
> ENABLE COMMUNITY SELF DETERMINATION
> AND ENVIRONMENTAL AMELIORATION."

It is natural to want to move up planes of existence – to have a better life for ourselves, for our children, and for future generations. This natural inclination has been a significant force behind our use, pursuit and consumption of energy. In much the same pattern, this natural inclination is becoming a significant force for more and more people across the globe. The so-called thirst for energy is not diminishing, but increasing at significant rates, and is taking place in a world that exhibits characteristics of social and political instability and unpredictability. It is this uncertainty that has added a new dimension to the conversations and concerns regarding energy. "Securing energy" has been added to previous notions of "economics" and "environmentally friendly." This latest dimension has brought with it a sense of urgency seemingly greater than that which accompanied previous (but still valid) concerns.

And so, as is our pattern relative to matters of existence, we look to technology to provide solutions to the energy issues before us, solutions which if they are to be ethically guided cannot be pursued in isolation from, but of necessity within, the context of the whole – the whole of humanity, the whole of life. Grounded in the current situation, ours and the world's, as a reality before us, and holding the aim, "to advance humanness... to enrich life – the life of the whole, and the whole of life on earth," we can, and by necessity will go forth. With a bit of thought we can see clearly that "stopping" or "putting a halt to" current human activity (tempting as it may be sometimes) is not a viable option. We can, however, go forth in increasingly ethical ways.

Bringing ethics and being ethical relative to our development and use of technology represents for all of us a true choice, a turning point... one that demands understanding beyond that which can be achieved through argumentation... a turning point, an imposed requirement if you like, that is lifted up by the ethical guideline: pursue technology and approaches that enable community self determination and environmental amelioration.

Community self determination offers the possibility to manage existence in a way that is open to and along the path of our potential, the path of intentionality, the path along which we can advance our humanness – move toward becoming fully and truly human. As humanness advances, peace – a particular manifestation of love at work within and among earth's people – becomes strengthened... and grows both in possibility and in realness of experience.

Environmental amelioration – bringing about an upward shift in our environmental state of being, an ongoing process of continuous improvement – takes us beyond just arresting run down, and brings into play enabling the work of run up, which in turn results in actions that reflect a deeper, more wholistic, more systemic understanding... actions that reflect more consciousness, and more ableness for being conscientious. And as our work to enrich the whole of life unfolds, harmony, the intended relationship between humankind, the community of life, the life processes of earth, and earth herself, also advances.

There is much hope in this turning point, this time of true choice, and this shifting of patterns.

Ethical Guideline Five

"CREATE PROCESSES THAT
ENGENDER UNDERSTANDING AND DISCOURAGE DIVISIVENESS."

It is natural for a life species, a life community, a life system, to bring or impose particular demands – real requirements for continuing their existence and well being – on the processes of life. As human beings we have inherently within, a developable capacity to understand the life community members' requirements, as well as to understand that which is required to sustain the vitality and viability of the processes of life, a capacity that is being called upon out of necessity – true need – for ourselves, for our children, for future generations, for the whole of life. This capacity is the very capacity required of us if we are to carry out a stewardship role upon and for earth, a role which cannot be filled as individuals, but rather as community... a community that can generate images of the wholes involved, the right and good - right for humanity, good for the whole of life

- working of each whole and the systemic nature of its working... a community that can create a process that generates understanding.

It is through understanding that true reconciliation can be achieved... a reconciliation that can elevate both human demands and life demands, two phenomena that often seem to oppose one another... a reconciliation that can bring into reality actions that simultaneously advance humanness and enrich life – the life of the whole, and the whole of life on earth.

This nature of understanding comes about through reflection and reflective dialogue. True reflection does not lend itself to (or in reality tolerate) the energies of argument, the energies that serve to divide. For the work of reflective processes is to gain understanding through the building of imagery – imagery coming from and working to create wholeness, a wholeness from which one can discover one's own role, one's work, the work of the heart.

And so what is seemingly being called for now is to take the energies of argument – the energies that are required to sustain the presence of a particular perspective or viewpoint – and transform them into willful actions of integration... willfully and reflectively ensuring that the particular perspective - its essence, its valuable contri-bution - is woven into the tapestry of the whole, thus enabling the community to generate and have access to wholeness and completeness of thought... and out from this living synergy of wisdom and reason, truth and knowledge, wise choices and conscious and conscien-tious decisions can be made.

Meditations on Wholeness

Wholeness is a manifestation of the working of truth. It is the experience of our inner being when we are open to truth - with the ultimate truth and the Source of all truth being love.

Wholeness is both a deep sense of connectedness to the Source, and an experiential understanding of the truth of our intended participation in the process of creation.

Wholeness is both a process and a manifestation of a process. It is a state of being that, while unlimited in scope and depth, deepens in meaning as our living and working become increasingly harmonious with our purpose and the core processes of our human and life communities.

Wholeness is not capture-able in the sense that we can possess it; in many ways, it is similar to the ebb and flow of the tides. We notice wholeness diminishes - it flows away from us - as we lose sight of the right and good working of the larger wholes of which we are a part: the human family, the whole of life. It retreats when we retreat into ourselves - particularly into the serving of ourselves. It flows into and through us as we remember and act from our instrumentality. It flows into and through us when we source our thoughts, and therefore the path we take, in our essential roles and purposes, and in the potential they offer to our becoming fully and truly human.

Wholeness is the work of the heart as it embraces both our oneness and our individuality; it reconciles and elevates both. It is what draws us toward and reveals more clearly the truth of our oneness and the reality of our uniqueness. Wholeness is the means by which we progress - as individuals, as communities, as the human family. It is a requirement for the taking on and fulfilling of our essential roles - roles within the human family, and roles within the whole of life.

Wholeness is achievable not through the resolution of differences, but rather in the pursuit of higher purposes, the celebration of uniqueness, and the manifestation of essences. If we individually or communally lose sight of higher purpose and pursue that other than essential purposes, wholeness dissipates. Wholeness is not about the imposition of one's will or perceived rights; it is about the surrendering to one's instrumentality... the instrumentality that lies within and emanates from the intent and design of the Creator.

PART 8 - SAYING YES

BEING INTEGRATION...
OUR WAY OF BECOMING WHOLE

The work for which we are now being called upon – the work for all children on the whole of this earth - is to bring about the being integration of humankind's essential virtue of compassion with the essential virtue of the land upon which we live and work... remembering the Source of both is the Creator. Holding both harmoniously and equally within our heart of hearts makes real the possibility of peace for humanity, and living in harmony with the processes of earth.

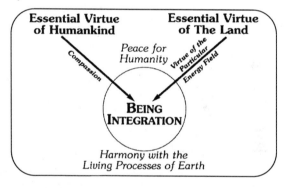

Reflecting on the image and its wholeness, seeing its right and good working, and understanding the systemic relatedness of its elements will, through inner processing and dialoguing, provide a means out of which can emerge planetary ethics, true planetary ethics – living principles that will enable our ways of living and working to be right and good for humanity, and equally right and good for earth, the whole of life, and all of its members.

Work and roles are the practical means by which these ethics become real for us... work and roles, understood and taken on, not only for ourselves, our families, and our communities, but also for the systems, processes and institutions critical for the healthy intentional working of humanity, and for the healthy intentional working of life itself.

Forming the Soul of Humanity

The manifested will of the Creator is actively and busily at work... tirelessly and unceasingly working to advance the work of the Creator. This work is work we cannot do, but work that cannot be done unless we are... are what we need to be such that spirit, and therefore love, can enter into and flow through the life processes of earth.

We are being called not to be in control of nor to have control over, but rather to cooperate with; not so much to lead, but rather to be led – led by the images that enter the heart receptive to wisdom and guided by the light of our conscience. This work demands unbending resolve and ever deepening patience on our part, for this work holds as its aim an unfolding with which we are fully able to cooperate. But also this work is one which we – as of yet – lack the capacity to fully envision, to see the whole, and the processes therein.

This is work not of the one, but of the many. Hope is active and entering all those with receptive hearts – hearts that long to become instruments, hearts that are striving to be free of the illusion of being the source. As hope enters and establishes its presence by flowing through, images and envisionments born of love become visible and accessible... images that make possible the seeing of our role – our path – and the clarifying of our work - work that is both a manifestation of essence, and the hopeful intent of our Creator.

While the whole of that which is to be brought about is not yet visible to us, what is being illuminated is the process of forming the soul of humanity. This is the work that is required for humankind – the human race – to become fully and truly human, and thereby capable of fulfilling its intended role in the working of the world. This soul forming work - this effort to prepare us for our intended role – calls upon the uniqueness of each and all, and requires the working and manifesting of spirit through our essence. This is the means; this is the process; this is the work before us.

Let us pray that we will not be tempted by illusions of "being the source," of being "in charge of," nor of having "control over." May our faith in the intent and design of the Creator ever strengthen and grow imperturbably within us. May we have the strength of resolve that becomes possible only through the desire to carry out "Thy Will." May the spirit and love of the Creator find ever increasing numbers of receptive hearts to enter and to flow through… such that the love required for manifesting the intentional unfolding is truly present.

GATHERING OUR COMMUNITY

Now is a good time to gather our community – our community of friends, family, colleagues, etc. - to read aloud, reflect on, and dialogue working for all children, moving towards wholeness... and away from that which divides.

...And as we gather, let us remember to be open to the seeing of roles... roles that are unique expressions of the work of our heart... roles that share a common character and presence... roles that come from a life of the whole perspective, seek to ensure love is present in the process, and trust that through reflection and dialogue the wisdom of potential will emerge... roles that come together to take up the work, the work for all children.

... And as we begin to see a way of taking up a role, let our spirits be lifted and our hearts filled with hope... and joy... brought about by this truth:

From the Creator flows love... and through love, all things are possible.